CHANGE WITHIN YOU

CHANGE WITHIN YOU

Dinesh K. Agarwal

ISPCK
Impacting Communities since 1710

2011

Change Within You – Published by The Rev. Dr. Ashish Amos of the Indian Society for Promoting Christian Knowledge (ISPCK), Post Box 1585, 1654 Madarsa Road, Kashmere Gate, Delhi-110006.

ISBN: 978-81-8465-136-2

Laser typeset by **ISPCK,**

Post Box 1585, 1654 Madarsa Road, Kashmere Gate, Delhi-110006, Tel: 23866323, Fax: 91-11-23865490.

e-mail–ashish@ispck.org.in • ella@ispck.org.in

website: www.ispck.org.in

*Dedicated
to all those
who lead others to Christ*

Contents

Acknowledgements

I am thankful to all those who helped and encouraged me to put in writing what I have preached on different occasions. The sources of stories and quotations are gratefully acknowledged and due credit is given. I am also thankful to Mar Geevarghese Coorilos, Wes Griffin and Samson Parekh for going through the manuscript and for giving me valuable suggestions and comments. Last but not the least, I am thankful to my family members for encouraging me to write this book and supporting me in my work.

Foreword

It is something remarkable to identify, bring and present the unchanging God in the changing world. The world is shocked at the frightening elements of deception, cheating, fear, death, etc. If they are stopped, it will be a wonderful experience not only to feel it, but also to bring unto others the Prince of peace, living and loving Christ, the Great Shepherd, God, who is good.

Bishop Dr. Dinesh K. Agarwal has a very unique talent for touching some of the unnoticed persons, themes and incidents. Amazingly, Bishop Agarwal can turn these unnoticed persons and incidents into individuals and events pleasing to God—persons and events that are of great use to humanity at large.

The emphasis on hope for a brighter future, the assurance of God's continuous presence and the relevance of deep faith in the Great Shepherd and the Prince of Peace is one of the unique contributions of Bishop Agarwal.

This book can change the reader's world view by

prompting him or her to see the light of the Lord within his or her heart. The thought in each sermon will encourage and challenge all of us to go deep into the presence of a living God, to underline the power of the Word of God as well as the fruit of the Holy Spirit and to face the challenge of today.

May the Almighty God bless Bishop Agarwal abundantly so that he writes many more books—works that bring the Good News to many. May the Holy Spirit guide him and the reader.

Metropolitan Geevarghese Mar Coorilos of Bombay
Malankara Orthodox Syrian Church and
Fmr. President,
National Council of Churches in India

Preface

My previous book, *Towards Spiritual Growth*, which consists of the sermons that I gave during my pastoral ministry, was published in 1992. Copies of this book were sent to some prominent church leaders, and I was encouraged by the response I received from them, but they wished that it should not have been abridged. So I kept their suggestion in mind. Nevertheless, the second edition of the book was published in 1999.

This book contains the sermons I gave from 1994, which is the beginning of my Episcopal ministry. Those who were blessed by the Word of God encouraged me to write the sermons down. I thought I would never be able to do it because of the pressure of work and engagement in administrative responsibilities, but the thought of putting them in writing was never abandoned.

This book does not include all the sermons I have given so far, but only those that I think are based on the life-changing events that occurred during Biblical times—events that have a powerful influence on our spiritual life and thinking. These Biblical events exert an influence on us because they deal with issues such as unbelief, spiritual emptiness, human sufferings and injustice. People from all church traditions and denominations across the world have been experiencing the power of the Word of God. Biblical events change us for the better; they bring about a spiritual transformation within us.

Basically, I have used the 'descriptive analytical' method in these sermons; which is not a widely used method in Biblical preaching. From the days of my Ph.D. work at the University of Bombay, I felt it was a great tool. A couple of years ago, I was invited to speak to students and faculty of one of the best-known theological colleges in India. I shared with them my spiritual experiences and thoughts on the principles of Biblical preaching as I had developed my own way of preaching the Word of God. After the seminar, I learnt that the professor of Biblical Preaching was very upset. It was not my intention to suggest that principles of preaching should not be followed. I believe, it is more important to preach the Word of God in the way you feel comfortable and yet remain faithful to Biblical truths, bring clarity and enthuse passion. After some months, I received the word from the college that the professor had reconciled to my approach to sermonising.

We often fail to notice the visible changes in the lives of our audience. It is simply because the preacher preaches the Word of God without first experiencing change within himself or herself. The preacher must experience the change first if he or she wishes to bring about a change in his or her audience. Even the best hermeneutical method for giving sermon will prove ineffective if this fact is not acknowledged. The Psalmist says: "Search me O God, and know my heart; test me and know my thoughts. See if there is any wicked way in me, and lead me in the way everlasting" (Ps. 139:23-24). These verses contain the key to effective sermonising.

I hope you will find this book useful for experiencing the change within you and for bringing about changes in others.

19 December 2009   **Dinesh K. Agarwal**

CHAPTER 1

Unchanging God and the Changing World

The world is undergoing vast changes. In fact, preceding centuries and millenniums experienced vast changes. Mankind has come a long way from the Stone Age to what is now known as the looming age, the electronic era, or the technological age. Interestingly, Daniel Bell, an American sociologist, speaks about the coming of post-industrial society. Nowadays changes are taking place at an accelerating rate. Heraclitus of Ephesus, a Greek weeping philosopher, said, "It was impossible to step in the same river twice, either the river has changed or we ourselves have changed. But God is eternal, invisible and unchanging. Paul wrote to Jewish Christians that Jesus is the same yesterday, today and forever. [1] Before reflecting on the unchanging nature of God, let us first look at the world events that are shaping our lives.

The Changing World

Unprecedented changes have transformed our lifestyle and thinking. Yogesh Atal, an Indian sociologist, rightly said that the 17th century was for mathematics, that the 18th century saw the rise of physical sciences and that the 19th century belonged to biological sciences. The 20th century can be regarded as the century of fear, and in the 21st century, fear continues to loom large.

We have witnessed incredible changes ever since 1989: Moscow's freedom revolution, South Africa's long walk, Tiananmen Square rebellion, Afghanistan's anti-Soviet jihad, Rushdie's banned book, etc.

The urge for German unity resulted in the breaking down of the Berlin Wall; the unification of Germany took place in 1990. No one thought that after the Russian Revolution in 1917, the USSR would break into independent states by 1992; and that the Marxist ideology would become ineffective and unattractive. Some scholars say that Karl Marx, German political philosopher, economist theorist and revolutionary, was confused about the dynamics of means of production and production relation. Hong Kong was restored to China by the British colonial rule in 1997. Other developments, such as Bill Gates' software technology, Wilmut's cloning experiments and spacewalk, are bound to affect mankind. Unlike the past, mass production, maximisation, specialisation and centralisation have led to mass consumption. The rapid rise of information technology, urbanisation, industrialisation and technological innovation has considerably transformed mankind in recent times.

We are amazed at the many scientific and hi-tech achievements of modern man—from land expedition and discoveries to space exploration and much more. Computer technology can enclose an encyclopaedia on a microchip. Israeli researchers packed the Hebrew Old Testament on a chip, smaller than a pinhead— 0.5 square millimetres. And, efforts are underway to make a match-sized mechanism to overpower gravitational force thereby eliminating use of elevators. The advancement in gene technology promises to reduce the aging process to make man live longer and disease-free. The development of alternate sources of energy, manufacturing of innovative superconductor devises to reduce significant wastage of electricity and the search for alternate and renewable raw materials due to steady depletion of natural resources will revolutionise man's life on our planet.

Unfortunately, the benefits of science and technology have not reached all so far. Poverty and deprivation are giving rise to Naxal-like tendencies. The resurgence of parochial and religious fundamentalist forces has been breeding terrorists. These developments are exposing us to greater risks, unprecedented security checks and changing geo-politics.

The global economy was looking good till recently, but the sudden economic downturn rendered millions around the world, desperate, jobless and poor. People are spending their energy on worrying about their future, consulting astrologers and fortune tellers rather than turning to the caring, living God. Some are losing their faith in the free market economy or *liassez-faire* system and its ability to restore good old days, but we shall overcome the present crises, for after darkness, comes sunshine. Apparently, change is experienced all over the world. It is pointing towards the way we should live and the way we should work with our economy. In his Book, *Third Wave*, Alvin Toffler, American influential author, scholar and contributor of management literature, says that there are other developments that create a similar phenomenon at the macro level. He says that in many countries, people are fed on a steady diet of bad news, disorder movies, apocalyptic stories and nightmare scenarios issued by prestigious think tanks; they have apparently concluded that today's society cannot be projected in the future, because there would not be any future. Certainly, we do not know what our future is going to be, but we do know who holds our future—the unchanging God. The Psalmist comforts us through his encouraging words: "Even though I walk through the darkest valley, I fear no evil; for You are with me." [2]

Unchanging God
Indeed, incredible changes are taking place, and in the future, more such changes may occur, but our God who brought back from the dead, our Lord Jesus Christ, the great Shepherd of the sheep is the same. [3] He is the Creator and Sustainer of all mankind. He is unchanging!

In His Words
Jesus spoke about the coming of the Kingdom of God at the end of this age. He said that the Son of Man shall come, but no one knows the time. However, He encouraged His disciples to be watchful. [4] He said as prelude to His Second Coming, there would be great persecution of those who believe in Jesus. There will be in fights in family; all will hate each other, many will be led astray from the faith in the Lord. The sun will be darkened, the moon will give up

its light, the stars will fall, and the powers in heaven will be shaken.

There shall be famines, earthquakes and wars between nations. When these things will happen, the 'Son of Man' shall come in clouds with great power and glory. On hearing this, Peter, James and John became inquisitive and began to ask Jesus in confidence, as when all these things will happen. Jesus told them to draw the lesson from a fig tree, but affirmed that all these shall happen before the second coming of the 'Son of Man'. Jesus said, heaven and earth shall pass away, but My words shall not pass away. [5] The pertinent question before us now is, whether the 'Son of Man' will find faith on the earth on His second coming? [6] A sustainable faith in the Lord will make all the difference and decide our destiny. Civilisations and circumstances do change, but His words shall never change.

In His Works

Jesus did many miracles and wonders. He healed the sick and fed the hungry. He gave sight to the blind and cast away demons. One of the special cases is Gerasene Demoniac. [7] Jesus walked on the water; Peter tried to walk on the water to reach Jesus, but when he noticed a stormy sea, he was frightened; he began to sink. He cried out, "Lord save me!" Jesus immediately reached out His hand and caught him saying, "You of little faith why did you doubt?" He raised Lazarus and Jairus' daughter from the dead. [8] We are not witnessing such miracles and wonders, because we doubt the power of God. Jesus said, "If you believe in Me, you also do the works I do, and indeed, will do greater works than these." [9]

Jesus taught with authority. [10] He finally gave His life as ransom for many. He said, "I came into the world not to be served but to serve." [11] The Scripture tells us that when you shall receive the power from above—the Holy Spirit—you shall be My witnesses. Many of us claim to witness Jesus, but without the power of the Holy Spirit. The disciples became powerful witnesses only when they were filled with the Holy Spirit; they did many wonders. The Holy Spirit is given to the Church; He will help us do works that need to be done for His glory.

In Love, Forgiveness and Mercy

He loved us in spite of our propensity for sin. The story of the prodigal son is significant in understanding the loving Lord. [12] Jesus gave a new insight into love. He asked, if you love those who love you, what reward do you have? Instead, Jesus said, love your enemies and pray for those who persecute you. [13] He prayed for His persecutors, "Father, forgive them for they do not know what they are doing." [14]

Today, we hear about the burning of churches and persecution of Christians; we need to pray for our persecutors. This is not the first time that the Church is facing such a situation, and this will not be the last one either. Historically, the Church grew in the midst of persecutions. In the early days of Independence of India, an unknown Indian political leader warned not to persecute the Church, or else it will grow like earthworms. We need to depend upon the mercy of our loving and forgiving God. King David, while responding to God's chastisement, said to Gad, his close associate, I am in great distress; let us fall into the hand of the Lord, for His mercy is great, but let me not fall into human hands. [15]

We need to depend on the mercy of the Lord; He will see us through in the time of trouble, for He is unchanging in His love, forgiveness and mercy. Surely, goodness and mercy shall follow us all the days of our lives.

The world continues to change, but God does not change; so we live. [16] This is the source of our joy and strength. Isaac Watt in his thought-provoking hymn, *O God our help in ages past,* wrote: "Under the shadow of Thy throne still may we dwell secure; sufficient is Thine arm alone, And our defence is sure [for] from everlasting Thou art [unchanging] God [alone]."

References: (1) Heb.13: 8 (2) Ps.23: 24 (3) Heb.13: 20 (4) Matt.24: 35ff (5) Matt. 24:35, Mk.13: 31 (6) Lk.18: 8 (7) Matt.8 (8) Jn.11 & Mk.5: 21ff (9) Jn.14: 12 (10) Mk.1: 22 (11) Mk.10: 45 (12) Lk.15; 11 (13) Matt.5: 44f (14) Lk.23: 34 (15) 2 Sam.24:14 (16) Mal. 3:6

CHAPTER 2

The Great Deception

Is there anyone who is above the danger of any kind of deception? Obviously, not. All of us have been facing the imminent danger of one kind or the other. Ralph Waldo Emerson, American Unitarian ordained minister and philosopher, says that deception means trickery or cunningness, the abomination of desolation is neither a burnt town nor a country wasted by war, but simply a discovery that the man who enthuses you upon celebration, or the man who favours you to achieve his ulterior motives. Those who want to make quick bucks, or gain position and power, or intentionally ditch someone by not keeping their words follow the ways of deception.

God made Adam and Eve in His own likeness or image and put them in the Garden of Eden to have fellowship. But Satan was unhappy about it; the Bible says that the serpent was crafty who deceived Eve; she led Adam to disobey God. They acquired the knowledge of good and bad because of their sin of disobedience. This is the great deception; the beginning of all deceptions. Satan is a skilful deceiver who leads the people of God systematically to deprive them of their God given spiritual inheritance. [1]

Misrepresentation

The great deception is the result of misrepresentation of God's Word. As God's Word is misrepresented, truth is deliberately hid; falsehood is amplified beyond recognition. The spiritual discernment brings out the truth like a lamp shining in the darkness. The Psalmist says: "Thy word is a lamp unto my feet." [2] There is an urgent need to study the Word of God to know its pure meaning in its true sense. The exegesis and exposition of the Word of God is a good way of understanding its meaning in its pure sense. The former discovers the truth, the latter unfolds it. The serpent misrepresented God's Word by adding, contradicting and transgressing it. The conversation between the serpent and the woman is intriguing, because the serpent systematically led the woman do what God has specifically forbidden to do, while making her feel good about it.

The serpent, a crafty animal, questioned the woman. Did God say, "You should not eat the fruit from any tree in the garden?" "No!" said the woman; we can eat the fruit of any tree in the garden, but not of the tree which is in the centre of the garden. God said, "You shall not even touch it lest you will die." The serpent took this opportunity to convince her that surely she will not die. The serpent said to her, God knows, the moment you eat it, your eyes will be opened; you will acquire the ability to know good and bad; you will be like God.

The serpent, by adding to the Word of God, made an irresistible offer. The woman saw that the fruit was good for food and tempting to eyes. She plucked it, ate; gave it to Adam. The serpent was successful in misrepresenting the Word of God by adding to it, to lead astray the first man and woman to disobey God's command.

The serpent said to the woman that she would be like God. She did the very thing that God had forbidden them to do. When God came to meet them, they hid themselves as they found themselves naked—not in the likeness of God.

The desire to feel important is the greatest craving in human beings. There is an intrinsic urge in every human being to become great, famous and rich. Many are lured, deceived by tempting offers sent through emails and SMS to become rich and famous. The early descendants of Adam were victims of the same, which led them into confusion. They were eager to make a big name for themselves by building the tower of Babel whose height would reach heaven. [3] On the contrary, Shadrach, Meshach and Abednego dared to disobey the order of King Nebuchadnezzar; even it meant to be thrown into a blazing furnace. [4] King Nebuchadnezzar made a golden statue; he commanded his subjects to bow down and worship it. They did not give up to pressure, although thrown in the fiery furnace. They came out safe from the furnace; the king believed in their God.

It was a bold affirmation of their faith that their god is not our God, but our God can become their God! Daniel refused to pray to King Darius. He prayed only to his own God, although he knew; he will be thrown into the den of lions. [5] Satan attempted to create doubt in Jesus, too, by boosting His ego that if He was the Son of God then He must throw Himself down, for angels will bear Him up.

But Jesus said to Satan, "Do not put the Lord your God to the test." [6]

The creatures of God cannot become the Creator of the creation. Man merely acquired the knowledge of good and evil by his sin of disobedience, which disabled him to know the purpose of God's creation. Man was made in the image of God to live forever, but because of his disobedience; he became spiritually dead; he shortened the span of his physical life as well. Remember, the Word was God; by the Word, the world came into existence—every thing in it. [7] The Word of God is like a mirror to those who read it; it is like a two-edged sword that discerns the thoughts and intentions of every man.

Succumb to Doubt

Man, the crown of God's creation yielded to doubt. Doubt is one of the deadliest weapons of the devil to lead astray people of God from the blissfulness. It has always plagued mankind. No one ever escaped from its influence, but some have overcome it by the power of the Holy Spirit. It is even being said about Mother Teresa, who is beatified as the Saint of the Gutter, that she, too, had a crisis of faith at times in her life. But remember that doubt makes mountains that faith can move! Satan used Eliphas, Bilad and Zophat, friends of Job, to pressurise him to curse God, but they were unsuccessful. Satan tempted Jesus on all the important aspects of man's life, such as hunger, position and power, but lost on all three counts.

God's Broken Image

The tragic result of the great deception is the broken image of God in man. The distinction between the image and likeness needs to be made. Irenaeus and Tertullian, the early church fathers, refer to the image of God to man's bodily nature, the likeness to his spiritual nature. The interpretation of the distinction between these two varied from time to time. The Alexandrians thought in terms of mental and moral perfections as compared with divine perfection.

In the middle ages, this interpretation led to a distinction between natural gifts of rationality and freedom. The distinction gave rise to explanation in terms of loss of grace; impairment of rationality and freedom. Man is made in the image of God, not to be the image of God. In other words, man is not to create God in his own image. Man is only a copy of the true image of God, but Jesus is the express image of God; the true original man.

The first man did not come in the presence of God or communicate with Him. Satan keeps tempting those who believe in the saving grace of Jesus. When we read the Bible, we hear God speaking to us; when we pray, we speak to God. Satan is very unhappy when people of God do this. He creates disturbances and hurdles for them. Sometime ago, a study was conducted to find out what Christians do on Sundays. One thousand samples were selected. It was found that 34 per cent watch TV, 38 .4 per cent go for picnic, 15 per cent pinch children during the worship service and only 12.6 per cent diligently worship the Lord.

The first man did not accept his own sin of disobedience, but blamed Eve for all that was done against the will of God. This tendency continues even today, everywhere. We pass the buck of our sins to others; we continue to blame others to conceal our own shortcomings and failures. We are not willing to confess our sins before God and people to receive the forgiveness of our sins. The Bible says if we earnestly confess our sins, God will forgive all our sins.

The moment the first man became disobedient, he gained self-consciousness; he lost God's consciousness. Self-consciousness is an instinct to listen to the voice of the devil; God consciousness is power to do the right things—things that please God and bring honour and glory to His holy name. Sin deactivates our conscience, the Holy Spirit activates it. Do not be deceived, have faith in God; let your faith be genuine and sustainable.

Jesus did the right things, though the Pharisees accused Him. The people of God from the Biblical times to the present history of the Church did the right things though they suffered for it. We, too, must do the same! It was never easy to do good; it is so even now. Satan is always there to see that those who do the right things are persecuted and punished. David prays, the Lord lead me in the path of righteousness—to do right things. Make your aim to hold on to your faith; rely on the Word of God, for the scripture is inspired by God and is useful for teaching, for reproof, for correction and for training in righteousness. [8] The scripture tells us, do not be deceived; God is not mocked, for you shall reap whatever you sow.

It is being said about the former world-champion chess player Paul Murphy, whose gaze was arrested by a peculiar picture while he was once visiting an art gallery. In this picture the artist had depicted a chessboard as a symbol of the game of life with the contest almost over. On one side, sat a young man with a look of despair on his face and on the other, sat a representation of Satan gloating over his helpless victim. Murphy looked intently at the picture for some time and then cried, "Bring me a chessboard; I can save him yet." [9] Remember God can save you from situations of deception and danger.

God wants to liberate you from all deceptions spread by Satan's representatives everywhere. Be watchful, do not be deceived; God is not mocked, for you reap whatever you sow. [10] Of course there are occasions when the people of God reap what they do not sow, but for His glory. Remember, God will not allow you to be tested beyond your strength and will provide the ability to endure it. [11]

References: (1) Rev.12: 9 (2) Ps.119: 105 (3) Gen.11: 4 (4) Dan. 3:16ff (5) Dan.6: 16 (6) Matt.4: 3 (7) Jn.1: 1 (8) 2Tim.3: 16 (9) Source: Decision (Magazine) (10) Gal.6: 7 (11) 1 Cor.10: 13

CHAPTER 3

Prince of Peace

Ever since the fall of man, peace became an elusive thing. Peace is one of the great words found both in the Old and New Testaments. Jews anticipated peace—David urges people to pray for peace in Jerusalem in one of his psalms. [1] Prophets foretold about the coming of the Prince of Peace—Isaiah called Jesus the Prince of Peace. [2] And, at the birth of Jesus, the angels with the multitude praised God in the highest; proclaimed peace and good will among men on the earth. [3]

The situation around the world is no better than before. There is growing disorder and discontentment among nations and within nations. No lasting peace can be found by conflict resolutions in the life of a nation, a family or an individual unless peace is experienced in the heart of people. We are living in the time of perpetual distress and alienation. We are witnessing economic exploitation of people and environment everywhere, rising rate of injustice and social problems such as broken families, drug abuse, etc. In spite of the progress we have made, the world remains a troublesome place to live in. But we are not without hope, on Christmas day; Jesus, the Prince of Peace, was born to give us peace.

The Early Disturbances

The promise of peace is found in God's love for the world. [4] The Scriptures tell us that in the beginning God made man and put him in the Garden of Eden. Everything was in abundance and order. He did not exploit nature, which was given to him by God under his stewardship. But this harmonious, peaceful co-existence did not last too long, as man was led astray to disobey God. The devil inflated man's ego and deceived him. In disguise, the devil lured the first woman and man to eat the forbidden fruit of the tree of knowledge of good and evil. They were misled to believe that they would be wise and equal to God.

But to their utter dismay, they acquired the sense of shame and guilt instead. They kept themselves away from the righteous God. The harmonious and peaceful condition vanished. Man could no longer meet God as before. Man was pushed out of the Garden to toil and earn his daily bread. This led to the spread of sinful activities.

Man began to kill his brother—Cain killed his brother; he refused to be his brother's keeper. [5] The younger bother robbed the birthright of the elder one — Jacob compelled his elder brother Esau to sell his birthright for a bread and lentil stew. [6] Man became selfish; he depended more on his own ability and strength than on God. The human family began to segregate (beginning from the Tower of Babel), giving rise to cultural diversity and early civilisation. [7] In the quest of 'this-worldly' goods, man began to indulge in exploitation and used unjust methods for amassing wealth.

Undoubtedly, the wealth of nations of the world is unevenly distributed. Economists and political philosophers are making constant efforts to bridge the gap between the haves and the have-nots, but the ideal situation is far off. There is a strong inclination to acquire new and remote parts of the earth in search of natural resources. Russia recently claimed parts of Antarctica, which was promptly denounced by other nations. The sinful act of man caused unjust distribution of natural resources, wars, concentration of political process and power in the hands of a few and human rights violations by denying the right to affirm faith in one true God.

Remember that Pharaoh refused to let people of Israel go and worship one living God. [8] God sent His only Son to bring peace on earth.

Agent of Peace

Peace cannot remain confined to history. Those who believe in Jesus must become the agents of peace. There are many peace-loving people in the Church who talk about peace but do nothing about it. God is looking out for peacemakers, not peace-loving people. Jesus said blessed are those who are peacemakers, for they shall be called children of God. We should be world peace leaders as we believe in Jesus, the Prince of Peace, but we are far from being such leaders. It is sad that there are disturbing conditions in the Church as well, which are not easily visible. There are people in churches who hold outward form of godliness, but deny its power; if it is not stopped, it will result in spiritual famine. It is painful to see so much of bitterness and hatred among the followers of Jesus, which is perpetuated by vested interests, creating and spreading harmful conditions for peace among us and in us.

Those who believe in His name must act as agents of peace. It is pathetic that there are not many people in churches today who dare to involve themselves in peace-making activities. Peace-making is not a one-time act, but a process; it begins within our hearts and gradually encircles the entire humanity. Peacemakers play a reconciliatory role without any desire to receive recognition or reward from man, but God alone. They do not sit on a fence, but engage themselves in creating conditions for the Prince to live in our hearts.

On the contrary, peace lovers desire to bring peace by remaining indifferent to Christian principles and practices. In all ages untiring efforts are made to bring peace on the earth, but without much success. God manifested His love by sending His only Son to bring peace on earth. We can experience it when the Prince of Peace takes birth in our hearts.

Christian peacemakers have a Christ-like character, which is built on Christ's values of love and forgiveness. When we face problems, we are restless and uneasy, but Jesus gives us peace. Jesus said to the woman, a sinner, who bathe His feet with her tears, your faith has saved you, go in peace. [9] Another woman, who suffered from haemorrhage for twelve years, touched the fringe of Jesus' clothes; He said to her, daughter, your faith has made you well; go in peace. [10] Jesus showed His disciples over and again how the healing touch can bring peace.

Indwelling of Peace
It is good to hold dialogue on peace and co-existence between religious, linguistic and racial communities and to

spread the message of peace among the people of the world; but it is not enough. What is more important and urgent is to experience the Prince of Peace within oneself unlike Herod the king. [11] This is critical to bring peace on earth. Everyone who believes in Jesus must experience the birth of the Prince of Peace within his own heart to reach out to those who are longing for peace.

When Christ enters our hearts, the process of restoration of peace begins. Christ revives peace in us by helping us to have peace with God. [12] The extent of peace and stability on earth depends on the extent to which the Prince of Peace is experienced by us. Jesus, the Prince of Peace, should perpetually dwell in our hearts. This is an unfailing way to bring peace on earth—all other ways, such as satyagrahas, the call for truth, religious tolerance and human sensitivity, stand next to it.

Let us not leave any stone unturned to bring peace on earth. Every effort made in this direction is important though it may not be sufficient. The distress conditions will cease to exist only when we experience blessings of the Prince of Peace. It is a reward that Jesus gives to all of us as we follow Him faithfully.

On Sunday, January 6, 1950, a young boy about 16 years of age was walking through a village street in a little town some fifty miles away from London. It was a bitter cold day, and the snow was falling heavily. He was anxious to find the peace of God, deeply conscious of his inner restlessness, breakdown, sin and failure of his life even at that young age. As he made his way through the streets with the snow falling, he felt it was too far to go to the church he intended to visit, so he walked back the lane and entered a little Methodist chapel. He sat on the back pew; it was as cold inside as outside. About thirteen people attended the church service. The 11 am service was five minutes late: the preacher could not reach the church on time due to bad weather. One of the local preachers came to the rescue; he began to conduct the service, and after a little while he announced his text: "Look unto me, and be ye saved, all the ends of the earth: for I am God, and there is none else." [13] In 10 minutes, he said all he knew about the text, and the service was over. The preacher, suddenly noticing the miserable and restless young man on the back pew, said to him, "Young man, you look miserable this morning, you need to look unto Jesus and be saved." The young man was none other than Charles Huddson Spurgeon, an influential preacher and evangelist who led thousands of people to Christ to experience peace within their hearts for forty long years.

The Prince of Peace gives everlasting peace to all troubled people of the world. Jesus said to His disciples who locked themselves in the upper room in utter confusion and fear, "I leave My peace with you; it is My own peace I leave with you. I do not give it as the world gives." [14] Simeon, a righteous and devout man, prayed to the Lord so that he may depart from the earthly home in peace according to God's Word. [15] The deepest and most universal desire of all men in all ages has been, "Grant us Thy peace O Lord, the Prince of peace!"

References: (1) Ps.122: 6 (2) Is.9: 6 (3) Lk. 2:14 (4) Jn.3: 16 (5) Gen. 4:8ff (6) Gen. 25:33f (7) Gen.11: 8ff (8) Ex.5: 2 (9) Lk. 7:50 (10) Lk.8: 48 (11) Matt.2: 16 (12) Eph.2: 13f (13) Is. 45:22 (14) Jn.14: 27f (15) Lk.2: 29

CHAPTER 4

You Must Be Born Anew

Jesus said to Nicodemus, he could not enter the Kingdom of God unless he is born again. Nicodemus was a member of Sanhedrin, a Pharisee, a ruler and a teacher of the Jews who went to meet Jesus at night, as he was unwilling to disclose his meeting with Jesus to his fellow Pharisees to preserve his eminent position or give any impression that he intended to become a committed disciple. [1] He genuinely acknowledged that Jesus was a teacher who came from God, for no one could do the signs that he did apart from the presence of God. He was deeply impressed by the profound teachings of Jesus; he wanted to know Jesus' thoughts on eternal life and supreme commandment of law, which were hotly debated among the scribes and Pharisees. [2] Jesus seized this opportunity and presented to him the truth concerning new birth. Jesus said to him that he can experience new birth and enter into the Kingdom of God if he is born of water and the spirit. Nicodemus did not understand even the basic of the kingdom of God although he was a teacher of Israel. He raised the question as to how anyone can be born after having grown old.

Nicodemus misunderstood Jesus' teaching on new birth. Jesus wanted Nicodemus not to perceive it in human terms. Jesus disclosed the truth that new birth is distinct or different from biological birth and that no one can enter the kingdom of God, no matter what his race or piety may be, apart from the experience of new birth. We can become children of God thought forgiveness of our inherent sin and adoption in Jesus, not by the strict observation of law or by racial privilege. [3] John used Nicodemus' dialogue with Jesus to tell us that we must be born from above to experience God's sovereignty in our life; all those who believe in Jesus must experience it, for no one can enter into the Kingdom of God without it.

Born of Water

Jesus said to Nicodemus, he could enter God's Kingdom if he would be born of water and the spirit. These two are important theological themes—water and the spirit. Water is one of the symbols of the Holy Spirit, but 'the born of water' here refers to John's baptism of repentance. It is used in a figurative sense of salvation of the Spirit by baptism and cleansing or sanctifying by the word of God. [4] Nicodemus was familiar only to John's baptism by water; baptism by the Spirit came to him as a surprise. The contrast between water baptism and the Spirit is found elsewhere in the gospel. The elements of cleansing and endowment are important in both John's baptism and Christian baptism. As a Pharisee, Nicodemus would not have submitted to John's baptism of water, which was the baptism of repentance.

Jesus said to His disciples that they were already cleansed by the word that He spoke to them; he cleansed or pruned them from every impurity of pride, misconception of the Messiah and eternal life. [5] This was not sacramental cleansing, but inner cleansing. The word of God is living and active, sharper than any two-edged sword, piercing to the division of soul and spirit, of joints and marrow, and discerning the thoughts and intentions of man's heart. [6] Jesus removed the hindrances that prevented His disciples to experience new birth and to enter into the kingdom of God. Jesus said to the Pharisees that it is the purity of heart matters, not of body. At water baptism, we publicly confess our faith in Jesus Christ, the son of the living God, and accept Him as our personal saviour and the Lord who died for our sins while we were sinner. The inner cleansing by the word of God leads us to repentance, forgiveness and regeneration in Jesus. The new birth radically changes our life and everything else around us.

Inner purity is critical for new birth. David longed for inner purity. He prayed to God to search him and find if there is any sin in him. [7] Jesus wanted the teachers of the Israelites and Pharisees, spiritual elites, to know this bottom-line truth. He said to them, you are only concerned about outward cleanliness; outward cleanliness is good, but it is more important to have inner cleanliness. The Bible says, God does not look at outward appearance, but the inside heart and mind of man. [8] Outward cleanliness is hygienic, but inner cleanliness is spiritual; it is the password to God's Kingdom. The word of God convicts us of our sins, leads to repentance and shows the urgency to seek first God's Kingdom and His righteousness.

Born of the Spirit
Jesus said to Nicodemus, he must be born of the Spirit as well; meaning indwelling of the Spirit of God. God's creative

power is not limited to material or physical things; it is also active in the spiritual realm. The word 'spirit' is translated in the Bible as breath or wind, or the supernatural energy of God. In Ezekiel's vision of the valley of dry bones, breath entered into the slain; they became alive. [9] The Scriptures tell us, when you hear the word of God and believe in Jesus as your personal Saviour and the Lord, you no longer remain under condemnation, but pass from death to life. [10] You no longer live by flesh or set your mind on the things of the flesh, for you become like those who live by the Spirit.

Everyone who is born of the Spirit is dead to sin and alive to Christ; he receives eternal life in Jesus as the free gift of God[11]. Those who are born of the Spirit give the greatest importance to Jesus, for the Bible says if you have the Son, you have life.

What does it profit a man if he gains the whole world and loses his own soul? [12] But, there are many who bid their souls for 'this worldly goods and power'. Jesus also answered the question raised by the young rich ruler, who asked him as what he must do to inherit eternal life. Jesus asked him to observe the commandments, but he said he had an excellent report card from his childhood. Jesus looked at him pitifully and said to him, you still lack one thing which is keeping you away from inheriting eternal life; go and sell all you have, and follow Me. [13]

Jesus said to Nicodemus that to inherit eternal life, one must be born of the Spirit; yield life to the Holy Spirit; live only for God and His glory; do the will of God as Christ did of His Father; remain under the absolute authority of the Holy Spirit; no longer pushing your own will, but the will of God who breathed His Spirit in you. The Holy Spirit leads a born-again Christian as the Shepherd leads his sheep, guides and enables him to decipher between right and wrong, prompts him to do right things and does not allow him to wash off his hands from the issues that promote ungodliness and injustice.

The Lord will open the door of the kingdom of God for those who are born again, not for those who are not born of water and the Spirit, though they may knock at the door of the Kingdom of God. The Lord will tell them, "Depart from me, you evildoers, for I do not know you." [14] Jesus said to Nicodemus, he must be born of water and the spirit to inherit eternal life. Nicodemus was merely inquisitive about eternal life, but lacked the will to take the next step to inherit it; may be his position and power prevented him to do so.

Understanding the Spiritual and the Physical
Nicodemus found it hard to grasp Jesus' words as he was trying to understand the spiritual by the physical laws. He mistook new birth for biological birth. He did not realise that he was attempting the impossible. It was like counting fish in a river; it is hard to know where to start, impossible to end.

Jesus removed Nicodemus' misunderstanding about eternal life, kingdom of God and superiority of the Mosaic Law and placed before him the urgency of being born from the above. He said to him, by looking at biological laws, he cannot experience new birth, but by faith in God. Jesus said that what is born of flesh is flesh; the wind blows where it chooses, and you hear the sound of it, but you do not know where it comes from and where it goes. So it is with everyone who is born of the Spirit. [15] The Bible says, by the sin of one man, death came into the world, but because of the death of Jesus on the Cross; death lost its power. The law could not do what Jesus did on the Cross.

The Body of Christ—the Church—is facing a gigantic problem. There is a tomb-like situation in it as it is looking out for extrinsic or material things. It is sad that the Church is grossly lost in the struggle over wealth and power, rapidly drifting away from the eternal and imperishable spiritual wealth of the word of God by choosing to walk on the broad way that leads to destruction. [16] Jesus said to Nicodemus to inherit eternal life or to enter into the Kingdom of God; he must be born of water and the Spirit; these are essential or critical conditions. The early church firmly believed in it and experienced the downpour of the Holy Spirit on the day of Pentecost. The power of God filled the early church in its fullness, transformed it into the likeness of Jesus, a new birth, and sent it as His mighty witness to the lost world.

The spirit of God caught hold of many individuals and raised them to an exceptional level of insight of activity beyond the scope of normal human capacity. Today, this is hardly seen in the Church; many Christians are not born of water and the spirit. There is no effective witness to our Lord within and without the Church. Evil forces are increasingly becoming active in the Church, aiming to lead astray the redeemed people of God who come together for worship and fellowship.

The teaching of Jesus on the new birth impressed Nicodemus, but he left without experiencing it. This must not be so with us; we must be born anew! The Church should strive unceasingly to help Christians to experience the new birth to enter the kingdom of God and bring others from all races and social groups to experience God's sovereignty. Let us confess our failures and sins at individual and church levels, forgiving one another, putting our confidence in Jesus—the High Priest of our salvation. The Holy Spirit will equip us to do so, if we remain faithful to Him, the one who has called us.

References: (1) Jn.3: 1 (2) Jn.3: 2 (3) Rom. 8:14-16, Eph.1: 5 (4) Jn.4: 14, Is. 12:3, Jn.15: 3 (5) JN.15:3 (6) Heb. 4:12 (7) Ps.139: 23 (8) 1Sam.16: 7 (9) Eze.37: 10 (10) Jn.5: 24 (11) Rom. 6:23 (12) Lk.9: 25 (13) Lk.18: 22ff (14) Lk.13: 25 (15) Jn.3: 6f (16) Matt.7:13

CHAPTER 5

Christ is Risen

The resurrection of our Lord Jesus Christ is a historical event that cannot be dismissed by any scientific theory or fractious story. The doctrine of resurrection is foreign to Hinduism and other religious faiths. They have nothing in common; so any comparison between cycle of rebirth and resurrection is illogical and irrelevant. The early church rightly understood and firmly believed in the Resurrection of Jesus.

When Paul wrote to Corinthians in AD 55-56, he stood closer to the fact of resurrection; his testimony is preserved in such a way that it is fresh to us as to his Corinthians Christians who had Jewish and Greek backgrounds. He referred to two great historical events: the resurrection, when God raised Jesus from the dead, and ascension, when God exalted Him to heaven over all forces of evil and made Him sit at the right hand, making all things subject to Him. This was a demonstration of God's power. The Church is built on the fact of the resurrection of Christ, for if there was no resurrection there could not have been hope.

Abraham's sacrifice of his son was an act of faith in the power of God to raise the dead. The mode of the death of Jesus, the Messiah, was foretold in the Scriptures. The bronze serpent in the wilderness signified that Jesus was to be lifted up as the lamb upon the Jewish altar. [1] The raising of Lazarus and Jairus' daughter are eschatological events that point towards the resurrection of Jesus. [2]

Central to Faith

The resurrection of Jesus is central to Christian faith; for, if Jesus was not raised from the dead as Sadducees and Epicureans claim, our faith would be in vain. If no dead person can be raised, Jesus would not be raised and our faith would be futile. [3] And those who have died in the Christian faith would have perished and those who are alive would be groping in the dark. The early church firmly believed that Jesus was raised from the dead. They preached Christ as the crucified and the resurrected Lord. They became martyr: Peter, Thomas, Paul, Stephen, James and others were killed for their faith. They would not have suffered death if they had not experienced the power of His.

Resurrection

A number of arguments are advanced to explain the phenomenon of the empty tomb. For example, there are some who say that the women came to the wrong tomb; they were told, He is not there, meaning He is in another tomb. Moreover, if it is so, then why did the women experience trembling, astonishment and fear? [4] John Chrysostom, a great preacher and the Bishop of Constantinople, said that some argue that grave-robbers had stolen the body because of time restraints and other difficulties. But this is not sustainable as the body was buried with myrrh, which glues the linen to the body not less firmly than lead. [5] It is significant to note that the grave clothes were undisturbed. [6] The gospel describes an orderly scene, not one of confusion; otherwise the grave clothes could have been torn from the body. This was something astonishing that took place as shown by the facts that the disciples saw and believed that the linen clothes lying; napkin which had been on His head was not lying with the linen clothes, but rolled up in the place by itself. [7]

The idea that Jesus' enemies removed His body is not better than a fairy tale. The tomb was sealed with a huge stone and guards kept watch over it. By taking away the body of Jesus they could have achieved nothing. On the contrary, by taking the body of Jesus, His enemies ironically could have posed big difficulties to themselves as to the Christians. But what is conclusive is the enemies' failure to produce the body when Jesus' followers began to make converts. They could have disproved the resurrection of Jesus once and for all if they had produced His body. This could have been a deathblow to the new sect. It is further said that the disciples of Jesus were in intimate love with Him; so they began to see Jesus appearing to them — an experience of hallucination? If this is so, then how come the resurrected Jesus appeared to five hundred, to James, to John and to others over a period of forty days? [8] It is impossible for so many people to experience hallucination at the same time. Hallucination is essentially a personal experience, not corporate; it tends to continue once it starts. There are some who say that Jesus did not die on the Cross, but revived in the coolness of the sepulchre. Any evidence, too, does not support this.

Post-Resurrection Appearances

Post-resurrection appearances confirm the fact of the resurrection. There are five written accounts—four in the gospel and one in Corinthians, chapter 15— that tell us about ten different resurrection appearances of Jesus to Jews. Five on the first day and five more spread over 40 days. The Scriptures tell that Jesus met Cleopas and others after His resurrection on the way to Emmaus. He stayed that night with them on their request; as they sat at the table, Jesus took the bread and blessed it, broke it and gave it to them to eat. By this they quickly recognised Him that He was Jesus. [9]

The disciples did not find hard to believe the evidence of their own eyes. He did not rebuke them or dazzle them with supernatural signs. He simply took some fish and ate it in front of them. Disciples were surprised into belief, coaxed back gently, rebuked by an utter natural and simple manner. After all, this was what they had seen Jesus do a thousand times. A ghost does not eat breakfast! This convinced them that Jesus was raised from the dead. [10]

They rushed to Jerusalem to share the news with others that Jesus Christ had been raised from the dead[11]. Thomas insisted on having a personal encounter with Jesus. Thomas said to other disciples, unless I see in His hands imprints of the nails, I put my hands into His side, I would not believe that He is raised. Was this, just a practical mindedness of Thomas? After eight days, Jesus again appeared to the disciples when Thomas was present. He called Thomas to reach out his finger, see His hands and place his hand into His side; Jesus asked him to be not unbelieving but believing. [12] Paul's Damascus experience of the risen Lord and his missionary commission led thousands to believe that Jesus was raised from the dead. [13] The news of the Resurrection began to spread like a wild fire from Jerusalem to Samaria and to the rest of the places. Since then, the Damascus effect has been experienced by many all over the world. Thus, weighing from the evidences, it proves beyond doubt that Jesus was raised indeed! And He is the first fruit of those who have fallen asleep! [14]

One of the claims of Jesus was that He is the resurrection and the life; those who believe in Him shall live, though they die. [15] Physical death is not the end for those who believe in Him; it is a beginning of a new kind of life in the same body. This is not to suggest the immortality of the soul—immortality only by the will of God; it is in no way close to the doctrine of transmigration of souls, which means that a soul of a man leaves his old body and enters into a new one. Resurrection is unique; our physical body will have the same physical identity with spiritual nature of the resurrected body of Jesus. [16]

Perishable and Imperishable

A question may be asked as to how dead bodies will be raised, especially of those who died thousands of years ago, either buried or swallowed up by the sea—or burnt by fire. By now they all must have turned into dust particles—undergone numerous changes. John Wesley, British clergyman and founder of Methodism, explained this in his writing on resurrection. He writes: "All the parts into which men's bodies are dissolved however they seem to us carelessly scattered over the face of the earth, are yet carefully laid up by God's wise disposal till the day of restoration of all things. They are preserved in the waters and fires, in birds and beasts, till the last trumpet shall summon them up to their former habitation… Therefore, the bodies of men being dust after death, it is no other than it was before, and the same power that at first was made it of dust, may as easily remake it when it is turned into dust again." [17] This may sound incredible, but not impossible for the Lord. [18]

There is a contrast between physical and spiritual bodies. The physical body made of flesh and blood will not inherit the Kingdom of God because it is perishable. Perishable and imperishable are incompatible. [19] The Scriptures tell us that a believer will have a glorious body like the resurrected body of the Lord. All those who died in Jesus Christ will come to life again on the day of His Second Coming, followed by those who did not. There will be resurrection of both believers and non-believers—even those who died before Christ. [20]

Resurrection manifests the power of life in Jesus. It points out that physical death and burial are like a seed planted in the soil. Death does not become a terror, but a transition. Nevertheless, the main aim of resurrection is the ultimate defeat of death as its final enemy. Life expectancy is increased due to better healthcare facilities, but death itself is not conquered, which Christ did on the Cross by laying down His own life through the act of redemption.

The Resurrection of Jesus is, therefore, a decisive beginning. It inaugurates the new age; it sends preachers out with renewed vitality and a message worth talking to the end of the earth to redeem people of the world from all ills. There could have been no good news if there was no atonement done on the Cross. Jesus suffered death on the Cross, for everyone; indeed risen from the dead on the third day! This is our faith and hope. All those who believe in Him should be dead to sin and alive to Jesus to transform the world in which we live. Only the experience of being crucified with Christ will help us experience the resurrected Lord and live forever for His glory. [21]

References: (1) Num. 21:9 (2) Jn. Chap. 11 & Lk.8: 40ff (3) 1 Cor. 15:14, 17 (4) Matt. 28:6 (5) Bromiley, Geoffrey, W. (Ed). "Resurrection of Jesus Christ" The International Standard Bible Encyclopaedia Vol. IV, Grand Rapids: William B. Eerdmans Publishing Company, 1991 p. 151 (6) Lk. 24: 12, Jn.20: 6ff (7) Jn. 20: 7 (8) Acts 1:3 (9) Lk. 24:31 (10) Guinness, Os In Two Minds", London: IVF Press, 1976 (11) Lk. 24:33 (12) Jn. 20:29 (13) Acts 19 (14) 1 Cor.15: 20 (15) Jn.11: 25 (16) Jn.20: 19ff (17) Wesley's Work, Vol. VII, Grand Rapids: Baker Book House, 1984 pp. 477- 478 (18) Gen. 18:14 (19) 1Cor. 15: 42ff (20) 1 Cor. 15:23 (21) Gal. 2:20

CHAPTER 6

Walk By Faith Not By Sight

A little boy was accompanying his father to see an exhibition. He was holding his father's hand while he was wading through the crowd at the large exhibition venue. He knew, the moment he would leave his father's hand, he would be lost in the crowd. He was, therefore, only looking at his father, clinging on to him. Walking by faith, not by sight signifies absolute reliance on the Lord without an iota of doubt; walking by faith in all the days of our life, whether it is sunshine or darkness. Thomas, the disciple of Jesus, was walking with the Lord, but he was not walking by faith in the Lord. He was overtaken by waves of doubt. He was walking with his mind like many of us, but not with his heart. Thomas is rightly called a twin, which may mean heroic and gloomy, but he was unable to influence the rest of the disciples with his own doubt—nor were the disciples able to expel Thomas' doubt.

Persistent Doubt

Thomas was not present when Jesus appeared to other disciples in the house, where they had assembled after hearing reports of His Resurrection. This was told to Thomas, but he did not believe them. He said to them unless I see the mark of the nails in His hands, put my finger in the mark of the nails, my hand in His side, I will not believe. [1] Thomas was not merely a follower or a believer of the Lord, but he was trying to overcome his doubt on the bodily Resurrection of the Lord — nothing is known whether he was influenced by Sadducees' teachings or thinking of giving them a befitting reply as they did not believe in Resurrection or angels, or spirits.

The stand taken by Thomas surprised all disciples. No doubt he was a seeker of the truth, but infected by doubt. He doubted the resurrection of the Lord and the cognitive ability of his fellow disciples as they failed to recognise Him. Probably, he recalled that on one occasion when the disciples saw Jesus coming towards them by walking on the sea, the disciples were terrified saying, "It is a ghost!" [2] They were under the spell of fear. Thomas knew that 500 people saw Jesus after His Resurrection, but this did not convince him. Thomas was a truth seeker and wanted to confirm the bodily resurrection of Jesus, but this act constituted the essence of his unbelief.

Thomas is one among many all over the world who are plunged into the darkness of doubt, unable to accept Jesus Christ as the only begotten Son of God. There are many in the worlds who are working overtime to prove that Jesus was just a good man. Dan Brown, American author, novelist and song writer, attempted to prove that Jesus was married to Mary Magdalene and led a normal family life. After analysing and interpreting the gospels, he turns to paintings by the famous Italian renaissance painter Leonardo da Vinci, including the paintings of the Lord's Supper (1495-97), in order to prove his view. [3]

Holger Kersten, a specialist in religious history, says that the Bible is silent on the life of Jesus from the age of 13 to 30 and after the event of crucifixion. The author gives a new interpretation of the various gospel accounts, including the Resurrection, to nullify it, based on unauthenticated evidences. He says Jesus escaped crucifixion. He tries to prove that Jesus spent some years in India and died in Kashmir in good old age. [4]

Rudolf Bultmann, a German theologian, said that Christian faith should focus less on historical Christ and more on transcendent Christ. He advocated demythologising the gospels. Shakespeare, British poet and playwright, said, "Our doubts are traitors, and make us lose the good we oft might win by fearing to attempt." [5]

Persistent doubt was messing up Thomas' faith in the Lord. So it does with so many of us today. We doubt God and His power for speedy delivery of justice when we are in trouble. One wonders why Thomas was not present along with other disciples when the Lord appeared to them the first time. Was he in despair? Or became very pessimistic about his future, or whether he was under the influence of Sadducees who did not believe in resurrection. Was he, therefore, now secluding himself from others? Although there are no ready answers to these questions, one thing is crystal clear that Thomas alone among the disciples was plunged into doubt. We meet people in church committees and conferences who always look out for the negative side of things like Thomas.

When Robert Fulton invented steamboat, he displayed his invention at the bank of Hudson River. There were some who were pessimistic and sceptic. They commented that the steamboat will never start; when it started, they said that it will never stop, but it did. Thomas wanted to see the resurrected Lord with his own eyes. Thomas needed to walk by faith more than his sight to believe in the resurrected Lord. For faith sees the invisible, believes the incredible and receives the impossible. [6]

Personal Experience

Thomas's dependence was more on God-given senses than God Himself. He was with the Lord for so long, yet he was far away from believing fully in Him. Thomas was all along living under the influence of pessimism. When the Lord said to His disciples, I go to prepare a place for you; I will come again to take you to Myself, Thomas at once retorted, "Lord we do not know where You are going. How can, we know the way?" [7] Thomas was willing to look forward, but still he was unable to see clearly.

Thomas set his mind against the post-resurrection appearances of Jesus as others began to speak more about them. One day, in the evening after a week, when the disciples locked themselves because of the fear of Jews, the Lord stood among them and said, "Peace be with you." Thomas was present at that time. The Lord showed to them His hands and sides, where He was nailed and pierced. [8] Of course, this was a very remarkable appearance of Jesus. The reaction of Thomas is interesting, as it reflects latent curiosity of each one of us caused by persistent doubt.

Jesus called Thomas to come forward. He said to him, put your finger here; see My hands; reach out your hand; put it in My side. Do not doubt, but believe! [9] Thomas stretched out his hand and put his finger in the nail prints of Jesus; he touched His side to verify that He was the same Jesus who was crucified and raised from the dead. He burst into the confession, "My Lord and my God." It took a while for Thomas to come to the point of no return. Jesus wanted to remove every doubt from the mind of Thomas who is known as twin or Didymus (Greek) and each of his disciples if they were to become His mighty witnesses. Jesus gave an opportunity to Peter too, who denied Him thrice. He restored him to full privileges of service again. Jesus only wants those who love Him to serve Him. If you love Him; you must serve Him. No one who loves Jesus can help but serve.

We often look at the negative side of Thomas who insisted on personal verification of the fact of the Resurrection of Jesus, but there is a positive aspect as well. After his confession, Thomas became a stronger follower of the Lord.

It was this first personal experience, it is believed, that led Thomas to come to India with the gospel. While he was praying, priests of Kali, a Hindu goddess, killed him by thrusting a spear into his back; he ran with it to the mountain that is now known as St. Thomas Mount, near Chennai (Madras), where he breathed his last.

Believing Is Seeing

I have often heard people say, 'seeing is believing'. Thomas also insisted on this practical principle. This is certainly a wise thing to do, but it does no good as far as our belief in

Jesus is concerned. Those who believe in Jesus must walk by faith, not by sight. A gentleman was addressing a reggae school in London on faith. Unable to understand, a little boy in the audience asked for an explanation. The gentleman said, 'Meet me at 10 o'clock tomorrow at King's Cross'. Punctually the boy appeared there. 'What do you want?' asked the gentleman. The boy replied, 'You asked me to come here, sir.' 'How did you know I would be here? asked the gentleman. The boy replied, 'I did not think you would deceive me, sir.' 'Well, my boy,' said the gentleman, 'that is faith.' [10]

Martin Luther, a great Protestant reformer, said, we are not saved by faith and works, but by a faith that works. People have experienced this over and over again. By faith Enoch did not experience death, Noah built the ark and Abraham set out from the city of Ur. He did not ask God to show him the place he needed to go before he actually moved out of his place. We are supposed to do the same all the time as we live a Christian life.

Jesus asked Thomas not to doubt, but believe. When we follow Jesus, we need to depend less on our senses and more on faith. Jesus said, by faith you can move mountains; see what God can do which cannot be done otherwise. Jesus said to Nicodemus, the wind blows where it chooses; you hear the sound of it, but you do not know where it comes from, or where it goes; yet you believe there is wind by its sound. [11] Thomas understood it while he confessed the Lord; not only seeing is believing but believing is also seeing. There was total change in the mindset of Thomas.

John tells us that Jesus did many signs in the presence of His disciples that are not written in the gospel, but whatever is written, it is written with the aim that you may believe that Jesus is the Messiah.

So walk by faith, not by sight. Of course, it is a blessed experience! Unlike Thomas, we are supposed to walk by faith, not by sight. There are people who believe in Jesus, but refuse to walk by faith. William Barclay, a distinguished British scholar and gifted preacher, said that the way to have certainty is to have the right kind of doubt. [12] Thomas tremblingly moved close to Jesus and raised his finger to put in the nail print of Jesus while Jesus gazed into his eyes, telling him not to walk by sight as others do, but to walk by faith in the Messiah, the Son of the Living God.

References: (1) Jn. 20:25 (2) Matt. 14:25-33 (3) Brown, Dan The Da Vinci Code (4) Kersten, Holger, Jesus Lived in India New Delhi: Penguin Books, 2001 (5) Measurer for Measure, Act I Scene 5 (6) Quotation by Susan Kirk taken from Decision (Magazine) (7) Jn. 14:5 (8) Jn.20: 20 (9) Jn. 20:27 (10) Story taken from, Christian Reader (11) Jn. 3:8 (12) Barclay, William, *The Masters Men*

CHAPTER 7

The Great Commission

Jesus gave the great invitation—come to me, all you are weary and are carrying heavy burden, and I will give you rest, [1] the great commandment—you shall love the Lord with all your heart and your neighbour as yourself, [2] and the great commission which is found in the first three Gospels. [3]

Jesus appeared to His disciples before His ascension into heaven and directed them to assemble at a mountain in Galilee—the name of the mountain is not mentioned. There was a clear division between those who believed Him as the resurrected Lord and those who doubted. Later, their doubt was turned into belief. This was the turning point in the life of the disciples, as henceforth the purpose of their life was to change. Earlier, Jesus called the twelve disciples and sent them out two by two to the house of Israel. But, now as a new Moses, He gave His disciples the great commission. It is great, because it is given to all those who follow Him and call by Him from all parts of the world to proclaim the message of salvation to the lost ones.

Authority

The great commission begins with the words: all authority in heaven and on earth has been given to Jesus. The New Testament word for authority is "exousia" meaning rightful, actual and unimpeded power to act or to possess, control, use, or dispose of something, or somebody. Jesus holds the spiritual authority as the Incarnate Son of God. The authority of Jesus is both personal because He Himself is God and delegated because He is the Son of God. God gave all power to His Son, our Lord. The power is all-inclusive; nothing is left out of His control. All things in heaven and on earth are subject to Him. The stars, the planets, the solar system, the galaxies and the whole universe are regulated in an orderly manner and are under His control. He set their laws; He alone has the power to change them.

The Centurion of Capernaum gave the best example of authority. The Centurion's servant was suffering from paralysis. He pleaded the Lord to heal his servant. Jesus said to him, "I will come and cure him." But the Centurion answered saying, I am not worthy to have You under my roof, but only speak a word and my servant will be healed. For, he said, I am a man with authority and there are soldiers under me. If I say to one go, he goes and to the other come, he comes. [4]

All things are under the authority of the Lord. Of course, Jesus has authority over diseases; He healed many. He had authority over demons; He cast out demons from those who were possessed. He had authority over natural forces; He walked on the water, rebuked winds and calmed the storm. He taught with authority and, above all, He had power to forgive sins. The disciples went out to preach the message of salvation to both Jews and Gentiles with the authority from the Lord. The High Priest and scribes could not bear to see such things happening because they could lose their both political influence and followers.

Jesus is the reflection of God's glory and the exact imprint of God's very being. He sustains all things by His powerful Word. [5] When Jesus appeared before Pilate, Pilate said to Him, do You not know that I have the power to release You, and the power to crucify You? But Jesus answered him saying, you would have no power unless God gave it to you. On the way to Caesarea Philippi, Jesus asked His disciples, what do you say that I Am? [6] Peter answered Him, you are the Messiah, the Son of the Living God. The Lord said to him, on this faith as a rock, I will build My church and nothing will prevail against it. The keys of the Kingdom of Heaven or God will be given to you. [7] Jesus gave the authority to the Church to proclaim the gospel to all people of the world, but unfortunately the Church is preoccupied with issues that are no issues and in fights on flimsy grounds. It is often observed that instead of using God-given authority to help people, it is used to destroy them. God expects us to use our authority for the edification of the Church.

Activity

"Go", is an action word found in the great commission. Jesus said all authority in heaven and on earth is given to Me, therefore, go and make disciples of all nations. The Church has mandate from the Lord to be missionary and not stationary. The preaching of the gospel is the foremost and the most urgent work of the Church. The world's population is over six billions, but not all have heard the massage of salvation as yet. The increase in the population is estimated at the rate of 17 to 20 per cent per year, but evangelistic efforts are lagging behind it. Certainly the evangelism explosion lags way behind the population explosion. The people of God must make continuous efforts to preach the gospel. Paul says, woe to me, if I do not preach the gospel. [8] There are many Jonahs in the Church who avoid going to the places that are difficult for preaching of the gospel. Many evangelists and preachers prefer to preach in their comfort zones. There are many pastors who chose to make parish as their world rather than making the world as their parish.

It is said about the founder of Mission to inland China, Hudson Taylor, that his life was a record of the power of God working through a delicate man until his mission was built with 5,000 workers who were filled with the Holy Spirit. A great crisis came in his life in 1885 when the task of millions of lost souls came upon him, but he could not take up this responsibility because of his ill heath. He wrote, "A million souls a month were dying in the land, dying without God. This was burned into my very soul." While he was in Brighton, walking along the sea, the Lord spoke to him that if he opens up China mission, he would carry out all the responsibility. He responded positively and found great relief in his heart. The China mission was founded on the spot; he became a new man spiritually and physically. [9]

There are so many missionary organisations with transparent vision to preach the gospel to the lost souls. Many are doing a commendable job, while others are merely exaggerating the statistical figures with selfish motives.

I recall when I was just a young seminary aspirant, I happened to spend some time with one pastor who claimed that he was doing great missionary work among the poor in certain backward areas. He was getting huge relief materials. It was shocking to see that he was simply giving relief material; baptising people by sprinkling Baptismal water over them as they stood in queue to collect some relief help. There was no preaching of the gospel of salvation. He was preparing statically exaggerated report with request for more financial support. It is unfortunate that there are some evangelistic organisations and individuals who are flourishing like smokeless industry while souls are perishing without hearing the massage of love and hope.

Go, is imperative, not an option. All those who experience the redemptive power of the gospel must go to tell others the stories, how the Lord has touched and transformed their lives. You must use the power of your personal experience of salvation to tell others how the Lord has saved you from the bondage of sin. Do not keep it to yourselves, but share with others. "Go", is therefore compulsion with conviction. The early church was filled with the power of the Holy Spirit; they could not curtail their movement; they were bubbling with joy; they stood firm as a rock to witness for the resurrected Lord. None could stop them; they went out from Jerusalem to Samaria to the remotest parts of the world. The entire experience was vibrant and transforming. The religious leaders of the time used their power and position to immobilise disciples, but with no effect.

Audacity

The Lord empowered His disciples with boldness to fulfil the great commission. He assured them that He would be with them while they commit themselves to the cause of the great commission. Jesus said, Lo, I am with you till end of the age. They were filled with the power of the Holy Spirit as the fulfilment of His assurance of His presence with them. They went out as His mighty witnesses all over the world; sharing the good news of salvation; caring not for their own life, but daring to confront those who opposed the preaching of the gospel; even at the risk of their own life.

Paul and Silas were imprisoned, because Paul cast the evil spirit from the girl, for the owner of the girl was making big money by using her for fortune telling. At midnight, a powerful earthquake shook the jail; the doors were opened and prisoners' chains were unfastened. On hearing it, the jailer wanted to kill himself, but Paul stopped him, saying we are all here. He knelt down before the disciples and he along with his entire household believed in the Lord. [10] The presence of the Holy Spirit was with the disciples as they went out from place to place to preach and teach the resurrected Lord, casting evil spirits and healing diseased ones. The evil spirits knew who the Lord's followers were and who pretenders were. The evil spirit questioned the seven sons of Sceva, a Jewish high priest, "Jesus I know, Paul , I know; but who you are?" [11]

When I was in the seminary, it was compulsory to do some practical work. I opted to work with one missionary organisation in rural parts of North India. I remember it was a very hot summer day. I was fully engrossed in giving gospel tracts to the people in the village. As I was walking along a canal, I saw a group of people sitting near the canal. I went to give them, too. I was a greatly shocked to see them suddenly spring at me, challenging me whether I believed in God who can save me if I was thrown into the canal.

I was alone and frightened, but soon I gathered strength to answer them boldly. When they saw I was not so much disturbed, they let me go with a warning not to come to their village again. I did not know at that time that one day, I will become a bishop and will be assigned an episcopal area that included the same village. There are numerous such stories of missionaries, evangelists and pastors the world over who took a great risk to preach the Gospel of salvation in strange and difficult lands, but the resurrected Lord remained with them to protect them from all dangers. The Lord is always with those who are committed to the cause of saving souls.

The great commission does not end with the spreading of the good news of salvation to the lost people of the world. But it also says baptise those who believe in the Lord, in the name of the Father, the Son and the Holy Spirit; teach them to do all that I command you. The disciplining is a vital part of the great commission. Jesus chose the ordinary fishermen of Galilee and He was continuously disciplining them as they followed Him wherever He went.

He led them into deeper spiritual experiences of the Kingdom of God through teachings, prayers, parables, signs and miracles. As a result of it, they were transformed into men of exceptional faith to face all the dangers in their life. These men who had fire in their heart went to different and difficult places with the simple gospel message that Jesus is the Messiah, the Son of the Living God who died for our sins, who was resurrected from the dead and who ascended into heaven, coming again to take us into heaven to live with Him for eternity.

Jonathan Lindell gives a lively account of a number of seventh- and eighteenth-century missionaries who travelled thousands of miles through the most dangerous routes to reach Nepal with the gospel. Many of them lost their lives; some of them were driven out of the country during the Rana regime and unification of Nepal. [12] This is one of the many mission stories around the world. A number of missionaries and evangelists in obedience to the great commission were imprisoned and tortured; they gave up their life joyfully for the sake of the gospel like the disciples, but even in that situation they fully believed that the Lord was with them. The great commission is not an option; its neglect would amount to defeating the very purpose for which the Church exits. Are we ready to give the account of our stewardship of the gospel on His second coming?

References: (1) Matt. 11:28 (2) Mk. 12:29ff (3) Matt. 28:18ff, Mk. 16:15 & Lk. 24:47f (4) Matt. 8:9 (5) Heb.1: 3 (6) Matt. 16:15 (7) Matt. 16:19 (8) 1Cor. 9:16 (9) Allen, William, How 25 Soul Winners Were Endued With Power , Revival Stories No.1, Rathfriland: Outlook Press, p.19 (10) Acts 16:25ff (11) Acts 19:15 (12) Lindell, Jonathan, Nepal and Gospel of God , Kathmandu: United Mission Press, 1997

CHAPTER 8

Neglect of Prayer and Preaching

A horse rider neglected to fix a loose nail in one of the shoes of his horse. When he made his horse run fast, the loose nail fell out. Unaware of the loss, the rider just kept spurring his horse on to run faster. The nails kept falling out and soon only one nail remained, which also got loose; the horseshoe slipped from the hoof and the horse fell over with the rider. Sometime a small neglect results in a big tragedy!

The disciples might have perceived that such a situation may develop in the Church if they neglected the ministry of prayer and preaching by taking upon themselves the responsibility of daily distribution of food to the widows and the poor in the early church. The disciples considered this as an important issue, but felt other people in the Church could take care of it who would be dedicated fully for it, while they continue to devote themselves to prayer and preaching. [1]

The disciples did not see any conflict between these two important functions—evangelism and social service. They are two sides of the same coin. After the day of Pentecost, as a result of earnest prayers and powerful preaching, there was a phenomenal response to the Gospel message. They were unanimous in their thinking that the proclamation of the gospel was of prime importance; greater attention was required and its neglect would defeat the purpose for which the Church exists.

Prayer
The Holy Spirit came upon the early church at a time when they were earnestly praying with one mind. Prayer is one of the most valuable weapons in the hands of the people of God which they often neglect to use. E. M. Bounds, American Methodist pastor, influential writer and profound thinker, said that the preacher who is feeble in prayer is feeble in life-giving forces; professional praying chills and kills both preaching and praying. [2] There cannot be any effective preaching without effective prayer. Churches all over the world must realise this.

Some years ago, I was in South Korea. My fellow Methodists took me to the Prayer Mountains. There are hundreds of tiny rooms in the mountains where people pray and meditate. The South Korean Church experienced a phenomenal church growth because they understood the importance of prayer in the work of preaching the Word of God. A large number of evangelists preach the gospel messages to people of other faiths; the preachers preach from church pulpits without first experiencing the power of the Holy Spirit. The preaching of the gospel to people of other faiths does not yield any fruit of repentance from sin, and the sheep in pews return home without receiving any spiritual food.

In the fall of 1802, John Hyde, as a young Presbyterian missionary, was on his way to India. A few hours after his ship had sailed out of the New York harbour, a letter was delivered to him from a friend of Hyde's father who wanted to become a missionary overseas, but was not permitted to go. The man had written to Hyde in care of the ship. We do not know the exact words, but the writer asked young Hyde if he had received the filling of the Holy Spirit, adding, "that is the great qualification for mission work." Hyde read the letter, crumpled it up in anger and threw it on the deck. A little later, better wisdom prevailed on him; he picked up the letter and read it again.

"Possibly", as he later reported, "I did need something which I had not yet received." He gave himself to prayers on the shipboard, which were finally answered in a marvellous way. He became known as 'Praying Hyde'. God used him in a great revival in Punjab. One man was filled with the Holy Spirit; the entire nation was touched.

The prayer is the power of the powerless people. Elijah prayed fervently. [3] Daniel prayed three times a day. [4] Our Lord gave importance to prayer. He always went to lonely places on mountainside to pray. He said to his disciples not to pray like the Pharisees did, but to pray in secret. [5] On the request of the disciples, He taught them to pray. The disciples earnestly prayed; they were filled with the power of the Holy Spirit. Prayer is vital to the effective proclamation of the gospel.

No soul can be freed from the clutches of satanic influence without the power of the Holy Spirit. The devil does not want the people of God to pray. He creates hindrances the moment they start praying, at times making them tired and sleepy. He makes the people of God despondent when answers to their prayers are not received as expected.

I, too, have the same experience. I used to make it a point to get up at 4 o'clock in the morning to pray, but whenever I faced a serious problem in my life and no immediate answers to my prayers came, I discontinued praying. There are many who have similar experiences. But you need to overcome it by defeating the tendency of despondency and committing yourself to prayer with renewed faith in the power of prayer.

Pablo Picasso, a celebrated French painter, said about his paintings that they could be used as defensive and offensive weapons to fight against the ills of our society. Prayer of people of God, too, acts just like this, nullifying the tricks of the devil that discourages use of the power of prayer.

Quite often, our prayers are quick-fix professionalism. One layman often complained against his pastor saying that his pastor's prayers were dull repetitions. Such prayers come out of a fixed mindset; they do not flow from the heart. You must spend time with the Lord in prayer till your prayers are answered. You must wrestle with God in prayer. Jacob prayed throughout the night. He did not stop wrestling with God although he was struck on his socket; his hip joint slipped, but he did not leave God till he was blessed. [6]

All great evangelists and preachers were great prayer warriors as well. Martin Luther, German Roman Catholic priest and the reformer and founder of the Lutheran Church said, "if I fail to spend two hours in prayer each morning, the devil gets the victory through the day. [7] Methodist Bishop Asbury said, "I propose to rise at 4 o'clock as often as I can; spend two hours in prayer and meditation."

John Wesley records in his journal: "Jan 1, 1739, Mr. Hall, Kinchin, Ingham, Whitefield, Hutchins, and my brother Charles, were present at our love-feast in Fetter Lane, with about sixty of our brethren. About three in the morning, as we continued our prayers, the power of God came mightily upon us and many of us cried out with exceeding joy, and many fell on the ground." [8] Do not give in to doubt, fear, unbelief and discouragement or use excuses for unbelief when your prayer is not answered immediately. Rebuke and resist all opposition to the answer of prayers and all suggestions of failure. So do not lose heart.

Preaching

The early church did not neglect preaching the resurrected Lord to those who had not heard about the gospel and to those who had accepted Jesus as their Lord and had become part of the Church. The early church preached the gospel not so much with homiletics principles—though they are important—but with truth, clarity and passion. Our Lord touched the lives of great evangelists who preached with deep conviction and courage of the Holy Spirit.

The life of a preacher is important whether he is preaching to people of other faiths or to those who are part of the Church, for preaching is the outflow of life hidden in

Christ. [9] E. M. Bounds says that a preacher is a golden pipe through which the divine oil flows. The pipe must not only be golden, but also open and flawless so that the oil may have a full, unhindered and unwasted flow. [10] A preacher who spends much time in prayer receives a message from God to free people from the bondage of sin. A preacher may be like Jonah who wanted to escape or like Peter who turned 5,000 people to Christ, but empowerment of the Holy Spirit is an absolute must. John Wesley said, "Make me O Lord a preacher who fears nothing but sin; desires nothing but God; such alone will shake the gates of hell and set up the Kingdom of Heaven on the earth." God does nothing but answer our prayers.

A sermon that is prepared on knees has a greater influence on the lives of people than the one that is merely prepared by head. I recall, at times, I preached all together different sermons on Sunday mornings than the ones that were prepared by the head alone. Preaching without prayer kills the sheep in the pews, but the preaching that is backed up by prayer wins souls for Christ. If we neglect to preach the gospel, souls will perish in sin, having no hope of eternal life. Paul said, "Woe is me if I do not preach the Gospel." [11]

All those who believe in the name of Jesus Christ must preach the gospel in season and out of season. [12] The early church preached nothing but the crucified Christ, bearing His wounds in its heart. Today, there are not many preachers who are anything but 'crucified with Christ'. The lifestyle of many preachers defeats the very purpose of the gospel. A number of evangelists and preachers of the gospel begin with great devotion to the Lord, but eventually become victims of the desire of the flesh, the desire of eyes and the pride in riches, for they do not have the life filled by the Holy Spirit. [13] Therefore, let us not preach so much by our words, but by our life.

The lives of so many Christians have become hindrance to the cause of the gospel. Mahatma Gandhi, an Indian proponent of non-violence, was driven close to the teaching of Jesus while he was in South Africa. Gandhi attended the services of a church in Pretoria. He later wrote: "The congregation did not strike me as being particularly religious; they were not an assembly of the devout souls, but appeared rather to be worldly-minded people going to church for recreation and in conformity with their custom." [14]

Little attention is paid to revival in the Church and church growth. We are pre-occupied and over-occupied with the maintenance of the Church's paraphernalia, which is paralysing evangelistic work and power-filled preaching in churches; promoting prayerless leaders like rainless clouds (cumulus). [15] The valuable time and money of the Church are spent on it, at the utter neglect of prayer and preaching. This loose nail in the Church's horseshoe causes spiritual famine and tends to undermine the power of the gospel message. Souls are perishing without hearing about the gospel. You, as the steward of the gospel, will be answerable to the Lord if you neglect prayer and preaching.

References: (1) Acts 6:1-6 (2) Bounds, E.M., Power Through Prayer , 27th Edition, London: Hunt, Barnard & Co. Ltd. P. 23 (3) 1 King 18:22f & Jam. 4: 16 (4) Dan. 6:10 (5) Matt. 6:5 (6) Gen. 32:22-32 (7) Ibid 1, p. 49 (8) Wesley's Work , Vol. I, op.cit. p. 170 (9) Col. 3:3 (10) Ibid (2), p. 11 (11) 1 Cor. 9:16 (12) 2 Tim. 4:2 (13) 1 Jn. 2:16 (14) Our Daily Bread, Jan-Dec. Vol. 8-02 (Aug. 5) (15) Jude 1

CHAPTER 9

Are You Available For God?

Our world is afflicted with many problems. There is always some problem or the other. World leaders are desperately trying to solve issues such as economic slowdown, nuclear proliferation, weapons of mass destruction, chemical and biological weapons, environmental degradation, terrorism and oppression of human freedom and rights. There are hosts of other problems including commercialisation of bodily organs. On the moral and spiritual fronts, there is decline of moral and spiritual standards, which denotes man's depravity in the midst of affluence. God is deeply concerned about this pathetic human condition. He is looking for those who will respond to His call to be available as a part of the solution.

The Call

God always sought persons who were ideally fit for His purpose. Abraham was called from the city of Ur to be the father of the nation, Moses was asked to lead Israelites out of Egypt, Joseph was sold as a slave to save his people from starvation at the time of famine and David was anointed as

king to lead the Israelites as a nation. Jesus chose ordinary
fishermen to be His disciples. Saul was sent to proclaim the
gospel message; hosts of missionaries and God's people the
world over are called to lead the Church in the midst of
crises and contagious wickedness.

Isaiah's call came in the vision where he saw the Lord
sitting on a throne, high and lofty; the helm of His robe
filled the temple. [1] Isaiah offered himself to be a prophet
to his people at the time when Judah committed sins against
the living God. Judah was politically and economically stable
for over 50 years during the reign of Uzziah, the king. After
the death of the king, Assyria's expansionist ambitious
scheme began to swell. In an attempt to thwart this danger,
Judah entered into an unholy alliance with the heathen king
resulting in a compromise.

God was not happy about it, as this clearly meant
limiting the power of the limitless God who gave victories
to Judah over their enemies. Judah was also practising
astrology and idolatry. [2] It was against this background
that Isaiah responded to God's call, which came to him in
a vision. His response was immediate and spontaneous:
"Here am I, Send me." [3]

In his vision, Isaiah saw the holiness of God and the
sinful condition of his people. He realised that neither he
nor the people among whom he lived were anywhere close
to God's expectation. [4] There was something more in
Isaiah. He considered himself unworthy of the mission of
God, despite his social standing. Isaiah had close contacts
with the royal family in Jerusalem. He realised that the real
source of his strength was God alone. So, Isaiah completely
depended on his simple and humble obedience to God.

Present Condition

Generally, prophets were raised during the dark days in the history of the Israelites. They were men of exceptional boldness who spoke against the sins of their day. They were chiefly concerned with the decline in moral standard and political corruption. It is true that the prophets were concerned with these issues, but the fact that people were worshipping idols was their greatest concern.

The condition of our present times resembles the days of Isaiah. The lifestyle of many Christians suggests that they are compromising with evil forces. Unholy compromises are common in the Church to gain power through church politics; moral and spiritual principles and justice are on the back burner. Once, my colleague bishop said to me that he would certainly help me, as I was in a crisis situation, if I take action against a certain pastor under my charge. I was shocked at his attitude, as I knew that the pastor he mentioned to me did nothing wrong to deserve any disciplinary action. He was merely vocal against the Bishop in business meetings for doing certain things contrary to rules. I did not agree with the Bishop. I could have avoided a lot of my problems, had I compromised with the Bishop, but then I could have harmed the pastor. There are no moral or spiritual principles when it comes to power; the only priority is to retain power and gain money. Jean Paul Sartre, French existentialist philosopher, has urged people to find a set of values or standards of some kind and commit themselves to it.

The lifestyle of many Christians does not show conformity with the Christian faith and teachings. Our newspapers and TV channels are flooded with the news of gory tales of murder, robbery, rape and terror. The glut of pornographic literature and X-rated films on the market is corrupting the young educated mind. Joseph was handsome and good looking; Potiphar's wife desired that Joseph should sleep with her, but he refused to yield to her wish as he was an upright man. She was very angry with Joseph for it. She accused him of indecency, and he was put in the prison. [5]

John the Baptist had been telling Herod the king that it was not lawful for him to live with his brother's wife. This was not taken well by the Herodian; she prompted her daughter to ask for John's head on a platter. The king was grieved, but he had to keep his oath before guests. John was beheaded in the prison; his head was given on a platter to the girl. [6]

Christians seem to be unduly worried about their future. Many Christians believe in astrology and influences of stones and stars. But remember, it is said, we do not know what our future is going to be, but we know who holds our future. What is the solution to this tide of wickedness that threatens to destroy all the good we cherish? Like Isaiah of old, we need to draw people back to a right understanding of God and his holiness.

There is growing a renewed interest in idol worship. These efforts are backed by the various organisations and corporate sectors in order to market their products. It is a challenge for Christians whether to identify with such organised events or remain exclusive to the God we believe in. It is a challenge because you have to pay the price of being exclusive in a pluralistic society, and it is an opportunity because you can tell about God you believe in.

Elijah was a great prophet whom God let loose upon wicked Ahab and idolatrous Israel. Jehovah sent him to do away with the awful worship of Baal during the reign of Ahab who was married to the wicked heathen princess, Jezebel. One day, Elijah suddenly appeared from the desert before the corrupt king and announced that there would be neither dew nor rain; there was no dew or rain for three and half years. [7]

The prophet asked the Israelites how long they would remain indecisive; he asked them to choose between Jehovah and Baal. He challenged the 450 prophets of Baal to pray to their god to bring fire on their sacrifice or he would pray to Jehovah to bring fire on his sacrifice. The prophets of Baal cried; they tortured themselves from morning till noon, but no answer came. Elijah prayed to God; fire came from heaven and consumed the sacrifice. When people saw it, they said, "The Lord indeed is God!" [8] It was an awesome sight that affirms the belief: Our is our God; their god cannot be our God.

Response

Today's situation is similar to the situation that existed in the past. Many people of God responded to God's call like Isaiah. Many dedicated missionaries and Christians have played a role similar to the one played by Isaiah.

The Sikh convert, Sadhu Sunder Singh, and the Brahmin converts, Pundita Ramabai and Chandra Leela, are some of those persons among others. Chandra Leela was born in a Brahmin family. After her mother's death, she accompanied her father on a pilgrimage to Jaganath temple—a Hindu deity. Chandra Leela's father died on the way, but she continued her pilgrimage. At the end of the pilgrimage, she was without peace. Later, she came in contact with Christian missionaries, accepted Christ as her personal Saviour and began to grow stronger in the Christian faith. Having found peace in Christ, she was inspired to share her faith with those who visited the places of pilgrimage. From the gateways of temples, she preached the message of salvation. The results were amazing! Thousands were led to Christ.

Christians are a minority in India. They are divided in various church denominations, but every obstacle must be viewed as an opportunity. It is true that the existing leadership and resources do not match the present pressing need of communicating the message of salvation and hope. But nothing should blur our vision of the great urgency of preaching the gospel to perishing souls. If we are to fulfil the missionary mandate in our time, men and women must make themselves available to God like Isaiah. This will turn the world, which is afflicted with so many problems, into a place of hope and blessing.

References: (1) Isa.6: 1-8 (2) Isa.2:6 (3) Isa.6:8 (4) Isa.6:5 (5) Gen. Chap. 39 (6) Matt.14: 8 (7) I King 17:1 (8) 1 King 18: 39

CHAPTER 10

For Me to Live Is Christ

S aul was a zealous Pharisee who became one of the ardent disciples of Jesus. He was greatly disturbed by the news that more and more Jews were accepting Jesus as their Lord and Saviour and joining the disciples; the Church was rapidly growing. He was bitter against the disciples. He wanted to stop them from preaching the risen Christ and do some harm to those who believed in His name. He approached the high priest and took the letters of authority to the synagogues at Damascus, so if he finds any one who belongs to the Way, he might bind him or her to bring them to Jerusalem to punish. As he was on his way to Damascus, suddenly the light from the sky flashed on him. He fell on the ground; he heard the voice: "Saul, Saul, why do you persecute Me?" He asked, "Who are you, Lord?" And, the reply came, "I am Jesus whom you are persecuting." Saul could see nothing; people led him to Damascus. After Ananias laid his hand on Saul, he regained his sight; later, he was baptised and filled with the Holy Spirit. [1] Saul from Taratus was transformed into Paul, who became the gospel brand ambassador with the mission statement: "For me to live is Christ." [2]

Sacrifice Self

Paul realised that if he was to live for Jesus, then he must not put the cart before the horse. He set his priorities right: Christ was before him; he was behind Him. This is a very rare quality found among some Christian leaders in the Church today. This was a charismatic change in Paul's life, which was brought about by the Holy Spirit.

There is a natural tendency in every human being to think first about himself. But when you are touched by the Lord, you no longer live a self-centred life; you live a Christ-centred life. Self-indulgence and self-enlargement are not the ways of Christians who believe in Jesus and live for Him. These tendencies lead us away from Christ, but self-sacrifice brings us closer to Him. The great philosophers of the past always said, know thyself; to free oneself from these tendencies by asking the question to yourself—Who am I? Where do I come from? Where am I going? In the life of Paul, self was no more dominant, but Christ was. He said, "It is no longer I who live, but Christ lives in me."

Once, I read a story about a lady missionary in China. The enemies of the Church caught her to behead her. When she got to the place where she was to be killed she burst out laughing. Her captors asked her why she was laughing. Is it a laughing matter to be put to death? She said that it gave her a great joy to sacrifice her life for the sake of the Lord, to share in His suffering by becoming like Him in His death. "Well," said the persecutors, "if that makes you joyful, why should we give that pleasure to you?" [3] Jesus said that those who want to save their life will lose it and those who lose their life for my sake will save it. [4]

John the Baptist, who was a fiery preacher, a great reformer of his day, accepted with all humility that he could never be a fruitful witness to the Lamb of God unless he acknowledged the supremacy of Jesus. He said, one who was coming after him is greater than him because He was before him; he is not even worthy to untie the thong of His sandal. He must increase and I must decrease! [5] Even the lifestyle of our Lord was self-sacrificing and self-giving, which is essential to live for Christ.

Count Others Better than Yourself
Paul warns Philippians Christians of the danger of a self-seeking attitude and pride—both of which could lead to harmful divisions in the Church. From time immemorial, the Church has been witnessing a tug-of-war situation on the issue of who's who in the Church. The opportunity to preach the gospel is lost; valuable time and God-given resources are wasted. There are some who take this seriously, but others do not. Our self-seeking attitude and pride must be crucified in us. Paul says, "I am being crucified with Christ; in fact, I do not live, but it is Christ who lives in me." [6]

There is need for self-realisation and confession—self-realisation that we have committed sin by our thought, word and deed and confession of our sins to receive forgiveness. Isaiah said, "Woe is me! I am lost, for I am a man of unclean lips; I live among a people of unclean lips." [7] Paul called himself a chief sinner. [8]

Jesus humbled himself, became obedient unto death. [9] Ah! Will not there be spiritual awakening in the Church if people of God follow the footsteps of Jesus? We need to practise humility in all spheres of our life. I often observed, humility and meekness are taken as synonymous. But they are not the same. Humility means unassuming, and meekness means not easily provoked to anger. Meekness is essentially a true view of one's self, expressing itself in attitude. [10]

Moses was trained in the skills of military warfare in the Pharaoh's palace. He was a strong man. One day he became angry; he killed an Egyptian. Of course, this is not meekness. He became a clumsy failure to deliver the Israelites with his own plan and power. He ran away from the Pharaoh's palace into the wilderness to learn the lesson of humility to be used by God. God trained him for 40 years in the desert. The Lord appeared to Moses in the flames of the burning bush; He asked him to go and deliver the Israelites from misery and oppression. But Moses said, "Who am I that I should go to Pharaoh to bring the Israelites out of Egypt?" [11] Remember, Peter reacted in a similar way. He pulled up his sword to resist those who came to arrest Jesus, but Jesus told him to put it down. Yet Peter became a meek man, a man tamed by the Holy Spirit under the control of God.

Paul had murderous intentions before his conversion, but when he was filled by the Holy Spirit, he became a great teacher of meekness. Oswald Chambers, influential preacher, said, "God can never make us wine if we object to the fingers he uses to crush us with. Moses was so much crushed by God that he became very humble more so than anyone else on the face of the earth." [12] It is fine to be competitive as far as it relates to proving one's technical skills and abilities, but the same must not be done when it comes to morality and spirituality. Paul says in humility, regard others better than yourself. I believe our world would experience change for better if we follow this spiritual advice. This is not a hard thing to do if we do not become judgmental. Jesus said to those who brought the woman who was caught in adultery to throw the first stone if there was any one among them who was not without any sin. [13]

When our pride of life turns into pride of Christ, we begin to count others better than ourselves. Satan knows that one of our weak points is our love for position and power. He did not even spare our Lord from this temptation. He said to Him, if you are the Son of God; turn these stones into bread.

A meek person shows tolerance to other people's views and feelings though it may not fit into his own frame of mind. He does not dismiss other people's views and feelings, but gives them due consideration and respect. He does not get easily provoked if his views are not accepted. You might think that meek and gentle people would not get anywhere in this hard world; everybody would ignore them, trample on them; it would be tough and overbearing to succeed in the struggle for existence! No, the condition for claiming spiritual inheritance in Christ is not might, but meekness. The Psalmist said, "The meek shall inherit the land and delight themselves in abundant prosperity." [14] Jesus said, "By meekness you can inherit the earth." [15]

Do Not Look at Your Interests

There is a blind spot in everyone's life. We cannot think and see the interests of others. In the competitive world, we tend to become insensitive to other people's interests. This is experienced in our day-to-day relationships and actions. The ripples of self-interest begin at the centre of our heart; they go to touch family, friends and colleagues; and the further they travel, the lesser we become aware of other people' interests.

Abraham, a great man of God, never thought about himself when he gave up himself in God's hand. He gave the first choice to Lot, his nephew, to choose between the plains of Jordan and the Land of Canaan. [16] Such are rare events among us. We often hear people claim: what is mine is mine, but what is yours is also mine. Our Lord did not think in this manner. Although he was in the form of God, He did not think himself equal to God. He took upon Himself the form of a man so that He could die for us on the Cross.

When you begin to live for Jesus every nook and corner of your life is filled with the presence of the Holy Spirit. Dwight L. Moody, a great evangelist and preacher, once used an object lesson to illustrate this truth. He raised an empty glass—empty except for the air in it—so that the people to whom he was speaking could see it. Then he asked, "Can anyone tell me how I can get the air out of this container?" Suck it out with a pump, one man suggested. No, Moody answered that would create vacuum and break the glass. There were other suggestions, none of them acceptable. Smiling, Moody picked up a pitcher of water and filled the glass. When water rose to the brim, he said, now all the air has been removed. So is the case with the Holy Spirit who enables us to become sensitive to the needs of others more than our own interest. [17]

Paul said breaking with the self-centred style of living is important. Many of us live for prosperity, career, a house full of gadgets, admiration from friends, tradition and rituals. He said that he had more reasons to live for these things, but I count them a loss for surpassing worth of knowing Christ my Lord, to love Him, to be found in Him and to gain Him. [18] The Damascus experience changed him once for all. The Damascus effect is felt by many around the world. It can make all the difference in your life as well.

A few years ago, we were shocked by the tragic death of Graham Staines, a medical missionary doctor from Australia, who lived for a number of years in the Eastern part of India. He was burnt alive in open market with his sons by Hindu fundamentalists. He is survived by his wife and daughter. Esther, Staines' daughter, said, "I praise the Lord that He found my father worthy to die for Him." There are many God's children around the world who laid down their life for Christ when they made their aim: for me to live is Christ. How about you?

References: (1) Acts 9:19 (2) Phil. 1:21 (3) Taken from "Our Daily Bread" (4) Lk. 9:24 (5) Jn.3: 30 (6) Gal.: 20 (7) Is. 6:5 (8) 1Tim.1: 15 (9) Phil.2: 8 (10) Jones, D. Martyn Lloyd, Studies in the Sermon of Mount , Grand Rapids: IVF Press (11) Ex.3: 11 (12) Num.12: 3 (13) Jn. 8:17 (14) Ps. 37:11 (15) Matt. 5:5 (16) Gen.13: 9 (17) Story by Anderson, Margaret J. Decision (Magazine), Oct. 1968 (18) Phil.3: 8f

CHAPTER 11

Cost of Discipleship

Everything has its cost. The diamond in an engagement ring costs more than the price indicated by the price tag. A miner has to risk his life to get into a diamond mine, look for the diamond and dig it out. A skilful craftsman cuts it, polishes it and embeds it in a ring before it is sent to the jeweller.

Discipleship, too, has its own cost. It is much larger than the twelve. Although, the twelve disciples formed the inner circle, but the gospels of Luke and John present the picture of a circle of disciples larger than the twelve. [1] Discipleship presents a personal relationship between Jesus and the twelve who were called by Him during His earthly ministry. Discipleship is open to all those who believe in Jesus and decide to follow Him in all circumstances. When the early church began to grow, many believers were added to it like us who became disciples of Jesus including Paul.

God prepares men and women for His ministry by internalising spiritual values in them, so that they can become a blessing to the world, but this does not happen without paying the cost of discipleship, which is beautifully put in a nutshell by the apostle Luke. [2]

Social Security
Luke tells us that the man who came to Jesus said, Sir, I will follow You where You will go. Luke does not give us the details of the conversation. But it can be seen from the response of Jesus that the man was intending to follow Jesus if there was a guarantee for his social security. Jesus perceiving his inner thought said to him, foxes have holes, birds of the air have nests, but the Son of Man has nowhere to lay His head. This shattered his hope of getting social security. He did not realise, like many of us in the service of the Lord, he would get such a response. In the past, people of God paid the cost by giving up their comforts.

After he predicted famine, Prophet Elijah was asked by God to go in hiding, where he was fed by ravens. [3] Many foreign missionaries reached our land to spread the gospel without first seeking social security; many of them worked in difficult conditions too. Social security should not become the pre-condition for God's servant. While Jesus sending His disciples on the gospel mission said to them, you received [the gospel] without payment, so give it without payment. [4] Take no gold or silver, or copper in your belts, no bag for your journey, or two tunics, or sandals, or staffs; for labourers deserve their food. Whichever town or village you enter, find out who is worthy and stay there until you leave. [5] Jesus was not teaching them to practise asceticism, but encouraging them to pay the cost for the sake of the gospel.

There are many who claim they are the Lord's servants,

travel by air and check in five-star hotels with credit cards in their pockets, but do nothing to spread the good news of salvation. Jesus said, such are not worthy for the Kingdom of God. Jesus said, first seek the Kingdom of God and His righteousness and all other things will be given to you as well. [6] The man who desired to follow Jesus had misplaced priorities. Jesus said, those who want to save their life lose it, but those who lose their life for My sake will save it. [7]

Sadhu Sunder Singh's story is remarkable. He is one of those persons who were set apart by the Lord for His ministry. He was a Sikh convert. Christian books used to make him angry. Once, Sadhu purchased a copy of the New Testament from his teacher; he inflamed it in fire. But Jesus appeared to him in a vision; he accepted the Lord and became His fervent follower. He faced many persecutions and humiliations from the hands of people, but remained steadfast in his calling. He travelled on foot for gospel mission in the Himalayan mountain in the most insecure condition. He never returned; no one knows for sure what happened to him. [8]

It is unfortunate that the so-called God's servants seek social security before serving the Lord. But there are others who first pay the cost of discipleship. I still hold the letter of appointment that was given to me as a Methodist preacher. In the appointment letter, it is written that I am being recognised as a worker of the Church, but without any housing and financial liabilities. It was a great challenge, as well as test of my faith in the Lord, but I gladly accepted it. The Lord did not leave me high and dry; He fulfilled all my needs.

Jesus knew that the man who wanted to follow Him was a fickle person. The Lord could have enabled him to accomplish greater things than what he hoped for had he not sought social security first before he could pay the cost of following Him. [9] David the king learnt from his experiences that the Lord does not withhold any good things from those who walk uprightly. [10]

It cost Jesus a lot to save us form our sins: He left the heavenly abode to live with us; he was born in a stable; he lived like any one of those who have no place to live; and he ultimately laid down His life for the sins of the world.

Set Apart

Another man said to Jesus, I want to follow You, but let me first bury my father who is dead. Jesus said to him, let the dead bury their dead, but as for you, go and proclaim the Kingdom of God. This was a very poor excuse on the part of the man. According to the Jewish custom, a dead person is buried on the same day of the death and no one would be following a teacher on that day. Interestingly, Jesus said to him, let the people who are spiritually dead bury their own dead, but as for you, set apart yourself for the ministry of the Word of God.

There are so many untold stories of people everywhere who left their homes and relatives to follow the Lord. The man was not prepared to pay the cost of separating himself from his family affection; although family concern is important, it should come only next to Jesus. It is urgent to preach the gospel; you should not waste your time and talent.

Jesus said, there is no one who has left his house or brothers or sisters or father or mother or children or fields for My sake who is not rewarded. [11] Jesus said, one who does the will of My Father he is My brother, sister or mother. [12] Jesus wanted him to separate himself first for preaching God's Kingdom and his righteousness. But he was giving more importance to the dead than the living. You should set apart yourself to proclaim the gospel, even at the cost of your life. Leave behind ungodly things and this worldly people to win souls for Jesus. Say no to the world, but yes to the Lord. There are Christians who had set themselves apart to proclaim the good news of salvation, left behind the so-called priorities and paid the cost of discipleship whole-heartedly and joyfully.

Influenced by the Christian faith, a Chitpavan Brahmin, decided to follow Jesus. He had unshakable faith in the Lord. It was hard for him to practise Christian faith in the midst of much persecution, but he did not forsake his mission. He came out of his community to serve the Lord. He made a tremendous impact on the Church through his poems. He is none other than Narayan Vaman Tilak, a well known Marathi poet and pastor. Those who set their mind on things of this world are not worthy to proclaim God's Kingdom.

Jesus set apart His disciples and sent them two by two to proclaim the Kingdom of God; they cared nothing for their life and laid down their life. Jesus knew that the man had a very feeble desire. He was avoiding the call to separate himself, making a lame excuse by saying, let me first go, bury my father and then I will come to follow you. Should we not know that there is no excuse for making an excuse in the service of the Lord?

Staying Power

There came yet another man who expressed his desire to follow Jesus. He said to him, I will follow You, but first let me say farewell to those at my home. Jesus said to him, "No one who puts a hand on the plough and looks back is fit for the Kingdom of God." The man lacked 'staying power'. Staying power means unwavering decision to focus on following Jesus. The Lord is looking out for those who have staying power for the cause of the Kingdom of God.

Even among the twelve, not all of them had staying power. Judas Iscariot betrayed, Peter denied, Thomas doubted and the rest returned to their fishing occupation, although Jesus expected them to be fishers of men—to bring out people from the forces of darkness. Following Jesus was marked by inconsistent commitment, failures and low expectation. James and John, sons of Zebbedee, requested Jesus to make them sit to His left and right in His glory, but Jesus said to them that they did not know what they were asking. [13] There are many who begin well to follow Jesus, but somewhere down the line turn back when they face hard times from the forces of darkness.

If you have a clear vision, it is not hard to follow Jesus. The shifting priorities do not help us keep looking at Jesus. There are many who took the first step forward to follow Jesus, but they could not keep it up focusing on Jesus. They met with failures when it came to proclaiming the Kingdom of God. Such followers do all things in the Church except seeking the Kingdom of God and His righteousness.

Joshua said to the people of Israel, fear not but go forward. [14] Paul said one thing I do: forgetting what lies behind and striving hard to go forward to what lies ahead.

[15] Jesus said to the man, focus your attention, keep following Me, look forward and do not look behind. We will be unworthy if we look back after we have put our hand on the plough of the gospel. We have not yet learnt to walk with the Lord, bearing His cross in sunshine and shadows.

The man thought that he will have a good time if he was on the winning side, but little did he realise that Jesus would ask him to pay the cost of discipleship. Give up all affections that become obstacles to preaching the gospel. David said, blessed is the man who does not get into the company of the ungodly. Paul was disciplining Timothy, exhorting him to practise scriptural holiness and shun unproductive conversation. [16] Follow Jesus in all situations and rekindle the gift within you to preach the Kingdom of God like a disciplined soldier, a skilled athlete and a hard-working farmer. [17]

Probably you heard the story of the tortoise and the rabbit. The rabbit boasted about his speed and challenged the tortoise to a race. The tortoise accepted the challenge. They appointed a fox as the judge. The race started and the tortoise kept going, slowly but steadily. But the rabbit sprinted off. He quickly left the tortoise far behind. As he was confident of wining the race, he decided to take a nap. By the time he woke up, he remembered the race and began to run, but the tortoise had already reached the finishing line. You need to keep focusing on the God-given Job after putting your hand on the plough of the gospel. You cannot afford to look back and take breaks till you reach the finishing line of your life.

The story of John Haggai, founder of Haggai Institute and leadership trainer for evangelism, should inspire us to pay the cost of discipleship. He said that God had put the fire in his bones for world evangelism. [18] He believes that the best method of evangelism is to train leaders the world over for effective evangelism. He paid the cost by giving up his comforts, hours of strenuous travels, planning and prayer. He, with his remarkable staying power, overcame opposition, impossible funding, frustrating negative responses and insurmountable obstacles, but it did work. Today, thousands in countries around the world are spreading the gospel message because of the man who paid the cost of his discipleship. Jesus said, whoever does not carry the cross and follow Me, cannot be My disciple. Should not we carry our cross and follow Him by paying the cost of discipleship? [19]

References: (1) Bromiley, Geoffery W. (ed.), op.cit., Vol. I, p 30 (2) Lk. 9:57- 62 (3) 1 King 17:6 (4) Matt. 10:8 (5) Matt. 10: 9-11 (6) Matt. 6:33 (7) Lk. 9:24 (8) Davey, Cyril J., Sadhu Sunder Singh , Kent: STL Books, 1980 (9) Eph. 3:20 (10) Ps.84: 11 (11) Matt.19: 29 (12) Matt. 12:50 (13) Mk. 10:37 (14) Ex. 14: 13 (15) Phil. 3:13 (16) 1Tim. 4:7 (17) 2 Tim. 1:6 & 2:3-6 (18) Haggai, John, The Leading Edge, Dallas: Word Publishing, 1988, p.30 (19) Lk. 14:27

CHAPTER 12

Fear Not, Go Forward

Fear is an unpleasant emotion. All mortals have an instinctive feeling of fear; it is aroused by exposure to some kind of danger. Fear threatens survival and disturbs peaceful existence. There can be fear of failing, unknown threat, unpreparedness, wrong decisions and rejection. We fear when we through some crises in our life or when we have done something contrary to established rules and norms, feel uneasy.

Some fears can be described while others can only be felt. There is also an imaginary fear that magnifies a problem. Fear can get out of hand; it can destroy happiness and relationships; it can also ruin someone's life.

Peter was walking on the water to reach Jesus in a boat, but he noticed a strong wind; he was frightened; he began to sink; he cried out, Lord saves me! Jesus immediately reached out His hand, caught him and said to him, you of little faith, why did you doubt? [1] Ever since the fall of man, fear affects everyone. But God gives courage to those who believe in Him, those who are in His plan. God said, fear not. Such assurances are found in the Bible.

Fear Not

There could have been no exodus or way out if the people of God had not left the land of Egypt and moved on to the land of Canaan. It was a very awesome and massive movement of six hundred thousands, besides children, flocks and herds. [2] And, what is noteworthy is that they were moving from bondage to freedom under the leadership of Moses. God entrusted this enormous task to Moses who was now a changed person, wholly dependent on God. D. L. Moody said that Moses spent 40 years in thinking that he was somebody, 40 years in learning that he was nobody and another 40 years in discovering what God can do with a nobody.

Moses was leading Israelites to the Promised Land. When they reached the Red Sea, they looked back and saw that the Egyptians were pursuing them with a strong army. The army consisted of 50,000 horsemen and 20,000 footmen. At the sight of this, the Israelites were taken over by grief and great fear. They began to accuse Moses for bringing them out of Egypt only to have their graves in the wilderness. But Moses said to the people, do not be afraid, stand firm; see today the deliverance of the Lord. [3] It was a moment of the great decision. They thought that if they did not listen to Moses, the powerful Egyptian army would slaughter them and that if they listened to Moses, they would be engulfed by the Red Sea.

It was a situation like 'damn if you do it' and 'damn if you do not do it'. But Moses was not trembling; he was strong in the Lord. He said to the people of Israel: Egyptians, you see today, you will see them no more, for the Lord will fight for you, but be patient and trust in the Lord.

Moses was cautioning the people of God not to overestimate the numerical strength of the Egyptian army and underestimate the power of God. Perhaps, he was also reminding them with unspoken words how God looked after them in the wilderness by providing food from heaven and water from the rock (bitter water was also turned into sweet water). Moses said to them, He is the same God who will give you victory over the Egyptians; do not oscillate in your faith in the Lord. By faith Moses left Egypt, unafraid of the king's anger, for he persevered as though he saw Him who is invisible. [4]

When they think of their destiny, many Christians get awfully frightened, as they see their bleak future. A man sees his own hopelessness, but God can change it into hope. There is no need for those who believe in Jesus to nurture fear. By judging from the events taking place in the Methodist Church in India, many predict that Methodist work in India will not survive for a long period of time. But I always told them while I lamented over ungodly things happening in the Church that it is the work of God; He will see through it as He did for more than 150 years. In the year 1856, the work of the Methodist Church was started under the leadership of Methodist missionary William Butler. In the following year, the first sermon was given to the first congregation with text from the gospel of St. Luke: "Fear not little flock for it is your father's good pleasure to give you the Kingdom." [5] Within ten minutes of the close of the sermon, the first war of independence broke out; the little flock was scattered and many of them were killed. But soon the Church began to grow and spread out—from the seed of the blood of martyrs.

Sometime ago, I heard a painful story of a new convert to Christianity. He said that when he was a follower of Sai Baba—an Indian god man who taught that everyone's Lord is the same—his business was flourishing; he had everything he needed. But ever since he accepted Christ, he lost everything. Today, he said, he does not have money on him even to pay the school fees of his children. He said that one wealthy Christian caused him immense misery for no fault of his. He said his only fault was that he respected him and believed him as a devoted Christian. He said the man and his whole family put all their weight to crush him. He said he had gone through so many sleepless nights in fear. He said he did not know what would happen to him. I told him that I too had undergone similar experiences.

I told him that a few days ago I picked up a copy of the New Testament and found a railway platform (station entry) ticket in it. Written on the back of the ticket were some Bible verses. I do not know who wrote them. One of the verses was from the book of Isaiah: "No weapon that is fashioned against you shall prosper." [6] If you are in God's plan, no harm will be done to you though for a little while you may suffer. You are not the only person who may be facing suffering; so many people of God are undergoing sufferings. Do not be afraid said the angel of God to Mary, the mother of Jesus, at Jesus' birth. After the resurrection Jesus said to His disciples, do not be afraid and at the time of His ascension He said to them; lo, I am with you till the end of the world. God was on the side of the Israelites and with Moses. Moses said to them, do not fear, but be calm to see the deliverance of God.

Go Forward

When the people of God saw the Red Sea before them and the Egyptian army behind, they cried out to Moses, but Moses was undisturbed and unmoved. He said to the people with deep conviction, do not fear, but go forward, for the Lord will fight for you. [7] But they were shaken, unsure of their destiny, wavering in their faith and unable to believe that the Lord is strong and mighty in the battle. [8] The Lord said to Moses, stretch out your staff over the Red sea; he did it and the sea was divided. Moses exhorted the people of God to pass through the sea. When the Egyptians saw that the Red Sea was divided and the Hebrews were passing through it, they became all the more furious, as their hope of keeping them back in the labour camps was crumbling.

They pursued them all the more vigorously to make them return to their work. As they reached the middle of the Red Sea, Moses stretched out his staff; the Red Sea returned to its normal depth, making the Egyptians perish in a watery grave, but the people of God walked on the dry ground through the Red Sea. [9]

There are people who believe in Jesus, but they have a shaky conviction in the power of the Almighty. They spend a lot of their time only on thinking about the positive and negative aspects of a matter; they spend a lot of their energy on worrying, but do not take the first step in faith to move forward. They are ready to reap fruits of faith without sowing faith in one true God. They are ready to be called heroes of faith without doing bravery work through faith in God. Let us remember, men of God of the present and the past conquered strongholds of evil by the twin forces of conviction and courage.

Going forward means breaking with the past. It is not so easy. There are many who resist such changes in their lives, although change may mean better things. God wanted the Israelites to follow Him and be exclusive people to Him, not assimilating religious values of the Canaanites or embracing the religious practices of the Egyptians. [10] The change from the familiar to the unfamiliar is not generally acceptable. The Israelites felt better in their comfort zone— Egyptian camps—rather than getting into the new situation. But if they were to enter into the Promised Land, they must go forward and break with the past.

The breaking with the past is a must. Of course, God does not want us to carry with us bitter memories and ungodly things of our past experiences. There is something to learn from the past, but it is inadvisable to lean on the past.

When the Lord was to destroy Sodom and Gomorrah, He was merciful to Lot, Abraham's nephew and his family. The angels of the Lord helped them physically, as they were hesitating to move out; they asked them not to look back, but Lot's wife running behind him looked back; she became a pillar of salt. [11] Jesus said to His disciples that anyone who puts his hand on the plough and looks back is not fit for the Kingdom of God. [12] Paul said, one thing I do, I press on, forgetting what lies behind and going forward to what lies ahead. [13]

The Lord led the Israelites from Egyptian bondage to freedom as they were a chosen race, a royal priesthood, a holy nation and God's own people in order to make them a great nation. They were called out of darkness into His marvellous light to remember and proclaim His mighty acts.

[14] The change was indispensable to claim the promise given by God to their forefathers.

You can go forward in the Lord without any fear when the Living God is with you. Your success without Him means nothing. Centuries ago, King Nebuchadnezzar of Babylon surveyed the great kingdom he had built; he saw in it evidence of his might and majesty. He said: Is not this great Babylon, which I have built for the house of the kingdom by the might of my power and for the honour of my majesty? In other words, the Most High rules in the kingdom of men, gives it to whomsoever He wills. God changed the mighty monarch into little more than a raging beast. Only when Nebuchadnezzar acknowledged the authority of God of heaven, he was allowed to return to his throne. [15]

The Pharaoh of Egypt refused the Israelites to go and worship Jehovah. The Lord hardened his heart only to prove His might. He raised and trained Moses to tell the people of Israel: fear not, go forward. God has a purpose for all of us; at times, we do not understand why we are surrounded by dark clouds. Even in such moments our eyes must be set on the Lord who leads us to the place where we do not want to go. Fear not, go forward as the Lord guides you in your life, for the Word of God says: "For surely I know the plans I have for you, says the Lord, plans for your welfare and not for harm, to give you a future with hope." [16]

References: (1) Matt. 14:31 (2) Ex.12: 38 (3) Ex.14: 13 (4) Heb. 11:27 (5) Lk.12: 32 (6) Is. 54:17 (7) Ex. 14:14 (8) Ps. 24:8 (9) Ex. 14:29 (10) Lev. 18:2ff (11) Gen: 19:26 (12) Lk.9: 62 (13) Phil. 3:13f (14) 1 Pet. 2:9 (15) Christianity Today (Magazine) Aug. 22, 1969, p.22 (16) Jer. 29:11

CHAPTER 13

The Great Shepherd

David, the psalmist, grew up as a shepherd boy. Initially, he assisted his brothers, but later took upon himself full responsibility of tending sheep. David was well acquainted with the geography of Palestine; he acquired the skill of tending sheep. He had a perfect picture of God as the Great Shepherd of all mankind. The psalms are not the work of his poetic imagination, although they have a great poetic value. In psalms, he penned down his understanding of God and his experiences with both God and man.

Psalm 23 is one of the most well-read psalms. The psalm is easy to understand, but to get a better picture of it, it is necessary to put it in its proper context. Psalm 22 is the psalm of the Cross, and Psalm 24 is the psalm of Jesus' coming, where Jesus is shown as the king—the chief shepherd of the sheep. But Psalm 23 is the psalm about the great shepherd of the sheep, Jesus the great shepherd of the sheep who loves and cares for all. [1]

Provider

It was not easy to find green pasture for sheep. The condition of draught and Rocky Mountains made extremely difficult for a shepherd to find green pastures and water for sheep. It seems, David took the cue from it as he held unshakable faith in the Almighty God who is the provider of all our needs. He was never in a hurry to grab position and power, but had intense desire to cling on to God, who is the provider of all things. King Saul thought of David as the enemy of his throne; he was craving to maintain it. But David's inclination was towards God alone. He learnt over a period of time from his experience of tending sheep not to get lost in what shepherd provides, but keep looking at the Shepherd who provides. A little boy was trying to correctly read the first verse of Psalms, but he read it as the Lord is my shepherd; He is all I want. This is the truth that shaped and guided the life of David.

Food and water are essential for the survival of all living. The psalmist sees God as the great Shepherd of sheep who provides these basic needs. The Psalmist wrote in Psalms: He makes me lie down in green pastures and leads me beside still waters. It is unfortunate that there are people in the world like Luke's rich fool who do not care for others. The rich fool accumulated as much grains as he could in his warehouses. Perhaps, he even sent his purchase officers to remote villages at the harvest time to buy grains from cash-starved farmers at much lower rates; he even extended his warehouses to store it. He was a self-seeking person who did not care for the poor and hungry in his neighbourhood. He flattered himself by saying: Well done! But the voice of the Lord came to him that his soul will be taken tonight. Unlike Abraham, he did not believe in God's providence.

Water is life sustaining. Two thirds of our planet is covered with water and yet there is a shortage of potable water in the world. A number of people around the world are suffering due to water-borne diseases. There is high-level wasteful water consumption everywhere. Water is emerging as one of the decisive political weapons in many countries. David firmly believed that God would lead us to streams of water in the midst of scarcity.

Hagar, the Egyptian slave woman, was sent out with Ishmael. She wondered at Beer-Sheba. There was no water in the skin (water bag made of animal skin). She thought that her son would certainly die due to thirst so she kept the child under a bush; she went away from him, for she could not see him die. But the voice from heaven came asking her to lift up the child; she opened her eyes and saw a well of water nearby. [2]

David believed in God's providence. He might have remembered while penning down the psalm how God provided food from heaven and water from the rock for the Israelites during their journey in the desert.

Some years ago, I received a letter requesting some help from an evangelist from North-East India. He was unknown to me, but I responded to his request. After some days, I got a response from him thanking me and informing me that by faith he and his family were waiting at their door for a postman. He wrote: We had nothing on us, but we believed that God would meet our needs, and there came the postman with a money order. David said young lions may suffer hunger, but those who seek the Lord will lack no good things. [3] Paul reminds us that God will fully satisfy every need of yours in Jesus. [4]

Restorer

David said that the Great Shepherd of the sheep restores life. Restoration means renewing and bringing back into the original state something of usefulness. The task of tending sheep is not so easy. It involves risks and dangers to both shepherd and sheep. When David offered himself to fight against Goliath, David convinced King Saul of his ability to fight with Goliath by telling the king how he rescued his sheep from the paw of a lion and the paw of a bear. [5] The great shepherd of the sheep is not the one who silently watches over His sheep while wild animals tear them into pieces.

King Saul was afraid of David because God was with him. [6] David was becoming more popular than Saul as he won many wars and defeated his enemies. People were praising David more than Saul. This was also adding to the King's fear that Jonathan, his son, may not succeed his throne. He began to act under the influence of fear of David; he decided to kill him despite the fact that David was his son-in-law. The plot to kill David was disclosed by the king's son Jonathan, a close friend of David, who advised him to leave the palace at once. David's wife Michal, too, helped him to flee from the palace. When the king came to know about it, he was very furious. This is not a strange and rare incident. History is full of such happenings. People have killed their father, brother and sister for the sake of gaining wealth, woman and power.

David believed that God would restore his situation. Saul was not happy when David was anointed as the King of Israel. He made several attempts to kill him, but was unsuccessful. When Saul learnt that David had fled away to the wilderness, he was very angry. He took along with him three thousand strong men to pursue and kill David. After extensive search, he was tired and exhausted; he wanted some rest so he went to the same cave where David and his men were hiding. David and his men hid in the inner part of the cave. David came to know about it. He took his friend Abishai with him to the place where Saul was sleeping, using a stone as his pillow. David stuck his spear in the ground next to his head.

As they were gazing over the King, men of David said to him, here is your enemy, do to him as it seems good to you. I believe at that moment David prayed silently, asking God to lead him in the path of righteousness. [7] Righteousness means doing the right thing. [8] It is not easy to do right things, more so in the Church than outside it. You face all kinds of oppositions if you walk in the path of righteousness which is unfortunate. It requires spiritual guts to do right things. But, don't be weary of doing right things, for God helps those who walk in the path of righteousness. David was a righteous man who responded to his men saying, I shall not raise my hand against the God's anointed one. [9] Unlike David, we wait to strike our enemies at first opportunity. When Saul came to know about it, he said to David, you are more righteous than I, for you have repaid me good whereas I have repaid you evil. [10] David was walking in the path of righteousness. He spared the life of Saul twice, although Saul was determined to kill him. He believed that power and position came from God in His own time. Today, such righteousness is rarely seen among the so-called church leaders. David was not in a hurry to sit on the throne of King Saul, but believed that the Lord would not hold back any good thing from those who walked uprightly. [11]

I know a church leader who had zero tolerance. If someone did not agree with him, he would go after him by adopting even unethical means to bring him down on to his knees. Of course, this type of attitude is undesirable. For, the Lord says: Vengeance is mine, I will repay. [12] If you want to hit a person a knockout blow, hit him with an act of loving-kindness. [13] Paul said by doing good to our enemies, we will heap burning coal on their heads. [14] But we feel that it would not work.

Protector
David firmly believed in God's protection. He had many near-death experiences, but God protected him throughout his life. David wholly depended on the Lord like sheep on its shepherd. A man's soul is more valuable than his body, but this does not mean that the body, in which the soul is caged, is evil.

Salvation is not the liberation of the soul from the bondage of the body, but forgiveness of sins in Jesus. God cares for both our soul and body, but the soul is more valuable. Jesus said, worry about your soul; not your body. Body fitness and beauty have now become a big concern, but the care of the soul must become bigger.

David knew that the Lord was with him; the Lord gave him great comfort and overflowing joy. He expressed it by describing 'overflowing of cup' and 'anointing of head with oil'. [15] David was a great sinner who became a great saint. It gave him boundless joy that God was dealing with a sinner like him so kindly. He was confident that even though his enemies may strike him or he goes through near-death experiences like going through the valley of shadow of death, he need not fear, for the Lord was with him. If the Lord guides our life like a shepherd guides his sheep on the right path, we will be protected from all dangers.

The concluding words of the psalm show David's passion for the house of the Lord. He wanted to build a house for the Lord and live in His presence. [16] But David was not allowed to build it as he was a soldier engaged in warfare throughout his life. [17] The Lord said to him through Prophet Nathan, you shall not build the house for me, but your offspring—Solomon shall build it. He expressed this unfulfilled desire in the psalm.

The psalm depicts the perfect picture of Palestine's life during the time of David. A shepherd leading his sheep was a common sight. The Great Shepherd of the sheep, our Lord Jesus, is going before us to guide our life; those who believe in Him follow the Great Shepherd of the sheep like the sheep follows its shepherd; behind them come goodness and mercy as rear guards to protect from all impending dangers throughout the journey of their life in this world.

References: (1) Heb. 13:20 (2) Gen. 21:8ff (3) Ps. 34:10 (4) Phil. 4:19 (5) 1 Sam. 17:37 (6) 1 Sam.18: 12 (7) Ps.23: 3 (8) 1 Jn. 3:7 (9) 1Sam. 24:6 &9 (10) 1Sam. 24:17 (11) Ps. 84:11 (12) Rom. 12: 19 & Deut. 32:35 (13) Quotation by John W. Welch, Decision (Magazine) (14) Rom. 12:20 (15) Ps. 23:5 (16) Ps. 84:10 (17) 2 Sam. 7:13 & 1 Chron.22:8

CHAPTER 14

The Cupbearer

Former President John F. Kennedy was the youngest president of America and a Roman Catholic by faith. Kennedy's youth, energy and charming family brought him world adulation and sparked the idealism of a generation, for whom the White House became 'Camelot'. In his inaugural address, he called on Americans to "ask not what your country can do for you, ask what you can do for your country." He was a motivating force and visionary who, while riding in a motorcade in Dallas, was assassinated. [1]

Nehemiah by profession was a cupbearer of King Artaxerxes. The kings' stepmother was Esther, the Jewess, who, no doubt, was still alive. It may have been that Nehemiah received his appointment through her influence. Nehemiah was the cupbearer of the king; the position was of trustworthiness and confidence. He lived in luxury and enjoyed the confidence of the king, but his heart longed for his people in Jerusalem, who were in agony and disgrace due to exile and destruction of much of the city. He was chosen by God, who gave him the vision to rebuild the wall of Jerusalem.

Vision to Rebuild

Vision is something seen other than the ordinary sight, or a dream; God's revelation to the prophets was usually through visions. The vision of Nehemiah was not his own creation, but was implanted by God. [2] It was not formulated in some leadership workshop; it was in his willingness to be used by God.

It is said that absence makes the heart grow fonder. In Nehemiah's case, out of sight did not mean out of mind. He learnt more about the condition of the people from every Jew who visited him at the Persian capital of Susa. Nehemiah was inquisitive about the happenings in Jerusalem. Perhaps, he enquired about every person he knew before he came to work in the king's palace. He heard about the pathetic condition in which Ezra the priest was conducting worship in the Jerusalem temple and ruin of the wall. He was far away from his hometown in the capital Susa, yet his heart was in Jerusalem—the holy city. [3]

He was grieved and broken down when he heard the tales of torment; he sat down and wept; he mourned for days, fasting and praying before God of heaven. [4] In such a time, God chose Nehemiah like any other prophet and men of God in the past and empowered him with the vision. Nehemiah's vision was not self-serving or for his own name and fame among his people; it was for the service of God and welfare of his people.

Prayer and Planning

Nehemiah realised that there were many roadblocks before him, but he believed that God would enable him to remove them. He was convinced that God wanted him to go to

Jerusalem to rebuild the ruined wall, but he did not have sufficient courage to spell it out to the king. Nehemiah's first reaction to the situation was not that of resentment. He did not blame anyone, but he knelt down and prayed to God Almighty, confessing the sins of Israel by not keeping the commandments and laws. [5] He had a genuine concern for his people, but wanted God to guide him. He prayed to God to find favour in the sight of the king. Our first reaction is always important when we are faced with problems, for we are better known by our reaction than action. Do we go the way of Nehemiah or do we pass the buck to others? We are often negative; seldom do we realise that sufferings bring opportunities for coming closer to God and for leaning on him to overcome sufferings. With suffering came the opportunity to Nehemiah to identify himself with his people, share their agony, live with them and work for them, which he always longed.

Nehemiah realized this could not have been possible without God's help though he was a deeply religious person. He wholly depended on God for his success. He did not push up his own planning strategies, but relied on God. It is good to have planning strategies, but they must come as an answer to our prayers.

One day he was serving wine to the king; the king noticed that Nehemiah was sad. The king asked him to reveal the cause of his sadness. He poured out his heart before the king; he told him about the destruction and disgrace of his people. He requested the king to send him to Jerusalem. The king gave him leave, a letter of authority and timbers to rebuild the gates. Such was the result of his earnest prayer.

The importance of prayer in planning must not be neglected. A session on strategic planning for the mission of the Church would hardly yield any result if it is not backed by prayers. Nehemiah, a civil governor, was empowered by the authority of the king to rebuild the wall of Jerusalem. Prayer and planning were an integral part of his humble service to God, which enhanced the quality of his leadership.

Mind to Work

After reaching Jerusalem, Nehemiah began to inspect and verify the things that had been pointed out to him. He along with other leaders began to take stock of the situation. A good leader always does this; he reaches a conclusion only after properly analysing and evaluating the situation.

Once I went with a senior pastor to inspect the hostel under my jurisdiction. It had come to my notice that the hostel condition was deteriorating despite the huge amount spent on the maintenance of the hostel. I had also come to know that hostel goods were being taken away. I inspected the hostel and found that the situation was as bad as had been reported. The new lady manger, who had been appointed by my predecessor, was the wife of a political heavyweight— a pastor. She had lodged a false complaint against me with the local police with the intention of blackmailing me. This created a great deal of unpleasantness in the Church, but the Church's ministry for underprivileged children and financial resources were saved.

Nehemiah began to articulate the God-given vision. He was a great team-builder; He was able to bring all classes of people together with the single goal to rebuild the wall of Jerusalem. This is a rare quality; some people have it. It is easy to remain as an institutional leader by the position we hold, but it is harder to be a people's leader. Nehemiah proved that he was a leader by the will of God, not a leader by virtue of his civil position in the king's palace. This enabled him to identify with all the people, helped him to bring them together and gave them a mind to work.

Nehemiah gave them a mind to work; he enabled them to see the need for contributing towards the work of rebuilding the wall of Jerusalem, which had been razed by the Babylonians in their conquest of the city over a century ago. The work was widespread, so he divided the work among different groups to expedite it to meet the deadlines. [6] In response to Nehemiah's appeal to rebuild the wall, the congregation at Jerusalem gave free labour and paid for the building materials. Such was the mind-set of the people—a mindset that could not be shaken by means of force.

Sanballat, Tobiah, Geshem and others opposed the rebuilding of the wall. [7] Opposition to this God-given job did not come from outside the congregation, but from within. This is often the case in today's institutional setting: inefficient people usually try to stop all good work by levelling false allegations against others. Some people are always very critical. This is killing the progressive spirit in the Church, discouraging initiatives for the extension of the Kingdom of God and depriving the poor and the needy of the benefits. Nehemiah chose to dismiss unproductive opposition. He stood firm against the opposition, fought with them with one voice and strength and completed the work. Such was his commitment to the work.

Water Gate Revival

When Nehemiah reached Jerusalem, Ezra had already been there for 13 years. Ezra was a priest; he taught people the word of God. Nehemiah withdrew himself from the scene after the rebuilding of the wall of Jerusalem was over; he let Ezra do his priestly duty. The people gathered to hear the word of God at the Water Gate. The Book of the Law of Moses was brought before the assembly; Ezra read out from it till midnight. [8] The people heard him very attentively from morning till night. The Word of God pierced the hearts of the people and they began to cry.

The revival broke out at the Water Gate Assembly because the Word of God was made central to all things. The focus was no more on individuals or on programmes, or on finances; it was on the Word of God. It is true that when the Word of God is made the reference point to all that we do in the Church, the Holy Spirit guides the Church. The Water Gate Revival changed the people, especially the way they lived. With confession and conviction they renewed their covenant with the One Living God, vowed to stay out of mixed marriages and resolved to observe the Sabbath and give tithes regularly.[9] If the Water Gate-like revival takes place in our churches, we would be bubbling in our heart to do God's will.

God used the cupbearer of the king, a civil governor, a real engineer and a layman, to rebuild the wall and repair the people's morals. Based on prayer and with undivided devotion, he completed the work. Nehemiah, a servant of God, sacrificed the luxury of the King's palace for the sake of God-given vision and completed the work without crediting himself.

Alfred Nobel, a Swedish chemist, engineer and industrialist, was a complex personality—both dynamic and reclusive. He was, in fact, a pacifist, but was labelled the 'merchant of death' for inventing explosives. It is said that he did not wish to be remembered after his death as a merchant of death. So, to counter this, he left most of his immense fortune to establish the Nobel Prize. [10] How do you want people to remember you after your death? Is it like Nehemiah? You must be like the cupbearer!

References: (1) Pappas, Theodore, Ed., op.cit., Vol. 5, p. 231 (2) Neh. 2:5 (3) Neh. 1:2 (4) Neh. 1:4 (5) Neh. 1:7ff (6) Neh. 4:19 (7) Neh. 6:1 (8) Neh.8:2ff (9) Neh. Chap.9 (10) Pappas, Theodore, Ed., op.cit., Vol.7, p. 121

CHAPTER 15

God Means Good

We do not understand God's purpose when we go through suffering or agony, or when we are denounced and rejected by our own. But the Word of God says that all things work together for good for those who love God. [1] Such a realisation does not come quickly, though it does come at the end when all things are over. There are many upright people in God's purpose who are undergoing suffering from the hands of those who became their enemies. Job had undergone such suffering as God wanted to show Satan that he was one of those few righteous men who followed Him uprightly.

Like Job, Joseph had to go through a lot of suffering, yet he never knew why he was going through it, till the end. He disclosed his identity to his brothers who out of jealousy treated him as their enemy. Joseph said to his brothers, do not be dismayed or feel bad because it is not you who sent me here, but God sent me before you to preserve for you a remnant on the earth. [2] Joseph wanted to count his blessings, not his troubles.

Tides of Crises

Joseph was going through tides of crises, but he was in the plan of God. He dreamt that his sheaf was above the sheaf of his brothers and they bow down to his sheaf. There was another dream, too, in which the sun, the moon and the stars were bowing down to him. When these dreams were revealed to his brothers and father, they were very much upset with him. His brothers did not take it lightly; they began to plan a conspiracy against him, but his father kept this in his mind. Joseph's brothers called him a dreamer; they conspired to kill him.

This kind of attitude is seen everywhere, even among the redeemed people of God. At times, some people cannot bear to see others grow in competence or do well. Jealousy breeds a feeling of anger, hatred, frustration and conspiracy; it arouses other negative human emotions. The reasons for such can be personal, popularity, competence, radicalism, deprivation and racism. Haman, enemy of Mordecai, intended evil for Mordecai, Easter's cousin, but he was hanged on the same gallows that he prepared for Mordecai. [3] A wrestler was so envious of Theagenes, the prince of wrestlers, that he could not be consoled in any way. After Theagenes died, his statue was installed in a public place; his envious antagonist went out every night and wrestled with it until one night he threw it; it fell on him and crushed him to death. [4]

Such things are happening in churches as well. Some leaders cannot tolerate the dedication plaques of their predecessors if they hate them; they remove the plaques out of jealousy. Joseph's brothers could no longer tolerate him; they planned to kill him first, but at the request of

Judah, his life was spared; he was sold for twenty pieces of silver to Midianite traders.[5]

Joseph became a slave, his feet were hurt with fetters, his neck was put in a collar of iron and he was dragged into the slave market. [6] The Potiphar, an official of Pharaoh, purchased Joseph. The Lord was with Joseph. He gained confidence of his master. Potiphar gave him control over all things except his wife. The official's wife desired that Joseph should sleep with her as he was very handsome. Joseph was a God-fearing man, a man of integrity. So he refused to listen to her in spite of repeated promptings. She became very angry with Joseph; she conspired against him. He was charged with misconduct and was put in the prison. But the Lord was with him, although he was facing problem after problem. It appeared that there was no end to his misery and suffering, but the Lord was with him. Many people find themselves in similar situations. Joseph was put in prison, but even in the prison he became a successful prisoner; he won the confidence of the jailor. [7] The jailor of the prison left everything under Joseph's control without any worry.

The king's chief baker and chief cupbearer were also imprisoned as they had displeased the king; they were kept in the same prison. One night both dreamt. When Joseph came to them in the morning, they shared their dreams with him. Joseph gave the interpretation of their dreams with the request to the chief cupbearer to remember him when he was restored to his position. He was restored to his position, but forgot to mention to the king about Joseph. He did not do anything to get him out of the prison. Such things do happen; people come to you pretending that they are your friends, but no sooner their self-interest is served than they leave you.

God uses people to help us at the time of our difficulties, just as he sends his angels to help his chosen people. You should always be grateful to those who have done some good things to you. It so happened by turn of events that the Pharaoh too dreamt, which disturbed him and made him restless. Egyptian magicians and wise men could not interpret his dream. The chief cupbearer realised his fault; he told the king about the young Hebrew who correctly interpreted his dreams. The king summoned Joseph; he interpreted his dream. Joseph also advised the Pharaoh to select a person who was discerning and wise to set him over the land of Egypt. [8]. But the king asked, "Can we find anyone else like this, one in whom the Spirit of God dwells?" [9]

Rise to Power

Joseph not only gave the right interpretation of the intriguing dream content of the Pharaoh, but also advised the king to take all emergency steps for providing food during seven years of dreaded famines. God raised Joseph second in command in the land of Egypt. Joseph was going through from one crisis to another from the time he was seventeen years old till he became an authority in the king's palace at the age of thirty. [10] Joseph was in crises for thirteen years; from pit to palace, but his faith in God did not shake.

We need to draw comfort from the fact that difficulties are not permanent when we face crises while we are in God's plan. Joseph was married to Asenath, the daughter of the priest of On. God gave Joseph authority over the land of Egypt. Joseph's brothers and others meant evil for him, but

God meant good for him. Joseph knew well that the Lord was with him. The Scriptures tell us that if God is with us, then no one can be against us. God rescues us as we go through from one crisis to another. No one becomes a successful follower of the Lord without first going through hard and difficult times. God turned every crisis in Joseph's life into a stepping-stone to raise him to be the power in the foreign land.

Joseph was endowed with wisdom and the ability to organise. He had the abilities of a super agronomist manager. He had excellent logistics of the gigantic project of food management. He stored up grain in abundance—like the sand of the sea; he stopped measuring it, for it was beyond measure. [11] Joseph was only a simple shepherd boy, but God raised him to be a powerful man in a foreign land and gave him exceptional managerial ability. The project involved various activities like purchases, transportation, building warehouses, storing grains, etc. It seems hundreds of thousands of people must have worked on the project throughout the land of Egypt. It was not easy to manage the men involved in the project over a period of fourteen years. But Joseph was successful as the Lord was with him in whatever he did.

When drought years began to roll out and affected the people, they came to Egypt to buy food. Joseph became the saviour of hundreds of thousands of people who otherwise could have died because of hunger. Many farmers in Vidharbha, Maharshtra, committed suicide due to severe drought and agricultural indebtedness. This is just a micro event as compared to the Egyptian drought. God used a dreamer boy who was hated, who was sold out to Medianite traders by his brothers and who did not know that he would save them and others from starvation and death.

Disclosing Identity

Joseph was well established in his authority in the land of Egypt and well settled in his family life. He wished to forget thirteen years of his bitter experiences as God began to bless him. The people from neighbouring nations came to Joseph to buy food due to severe seven years of famine. It so happened that his father sent his brothers to Egypt to buy food. Joseph recognised them, but they did not even have a stretch of imagination that the person in authority could be their own brother whom they hated due to jealousy; they sold him to Medianite traders out of anger. Joseph was very keen to know about his father and his brother Benjamin. He did not hold his brothers or other responsible for his sufferings. He realised that God had sent him before them to Egypt to save them from death by starvation.

I was surprised to receive telephone calls from my conspirators some time ago, asking for an apology to what they had done against me. My simple response was, "I do not want to remember the past; I do not blame any one for all that I am going through."

It was an emotion-packed event when Joseph began to disclose his identity to his brothers. He sent them back with grain to bring Benjamin, his brother, the son of his own mother, Rachel. When Joseph saw Benjamin, he was overjoyed; he ordered his servants to prepare a feast in his honour. His brothers carried into his house gifts and bowed before him. His dream came true, but he could not control his emotion. He went aside as he was about to cry after he saw his brother Benjamin whom he loved so much. [12] Benjamin was detained in spite of the pleading by his brothers. Joseph could no longer hold back his identity from his brothers; he sent out everyone who stood by him; he cried so loudly that even the Egyptians could hear him. Joseph said to his brothers, "I am Joseph. Is my father still alive?" But his brothers were taken aback; they became shameful and speechless; and they thought he would be vindictive. But he called his brothers closer to him and said to them, I am your brother Joseph whom you sold to the Medianite traders. Do not be distressed or angry with yourselves, because you sold me here, for God sent me before you to preserve life. [13] Is this not true with many of our situations today? Let us realise that God means good for us when we face a similar situation.

References: (1) Rom.8: 28 (2) Gen.45: 7 (3) Esther 7:10 (4) Doran's Minister's Manual, p.87 (5) Gen. 37:26 (6) Ps. 105:17-18 (7) Gen.39: 22 (8) Gen.41: 33 (9) Gen.41: 38 (10) Gen.37: 2 & 41:46 (11) Gen. 41:49 (12) Gen. 43:30 (13) Gen. 45:5

CHAPTER 16

God's Dream for You

Madame Marie Curie, a French chemist, did very extensive research in the area of radioactivity. She knew her research in the area of radioactivity was potentially very risky, but she along with her husband, who was an equally eminent scientist, laboured tirelessly. She hoped that her research in some way could help humanity, but she did not know that in coming days it will be used to bring cheer to cancer patients. She lost her husband, but kept her dream alive by continuing her research, though it was unsafe. At last she was successful in distinguishing alpha, beta and gamma radiation. She was honoured with two Nobel Prizes for her work on discovery of polonium and isolating radium. It is sad that she died of leukaemia caused by her prolong exposure to radioactivity. Our living God, too, dreamt for you to save you from sins although it meant sending His only Son, Jesus, to die on the Cross for the sins of the whole world.

He Visualised in Jesus

The first three chapters of the Bible are very important as they tell us about the creation and fall of man. Everything follows it—tells about God's dream to restore His broken image in man as the crown of creation. God's dream is all about restoring the broken image, bringing back man in His fold and defeating Satan. God said to the serpent, "I will put enmity between you and the woman and between your offspring and hers; he will strike your head; you will strike his heel." [1]

God, in His eternal purpose, did not wish man to live separately from Him, alienated from eternal life. Out of His immense love, He planned to forgive his sins in His Son, our Lord Jesus. God made man in His own image, but due to the fall of man, the image of God in man was broken. The restoration of the image of God in man was the dream to be fulfilled. God said: Let Us make humankind in Our image according to Our likeness, so He made man in his own image. [2]

The forgiveness of our sins was made possible by the shedding of the blood of Jesus on the Cross; it was not otherwise possible to obtain salvation by the observation of the laws or continuous offering of Levitical sacrifices. Jesus offered sacrifice of Himself, once for all, to forgive and cleanse us from our sins. [3]

God chose us to live a holy and blameless life. But many of us are not clear about it. We often think that we have chosen Jesus to follow Him, but this is not so. Jesus, the Saviour of the world, saved us and chose us so that we may live a holy and blameless life in Him. This is a great opportunity and challenge; it is an opportunity because we are called to live a holy and blameless life; it is a challenge because we cannot do it without God's righteousness. We are special in the sight of God because He chose us out of this world. He chose the foolish and the poor of the world to make them wise and rich in Him.

God chose us out of the world before the foundation of the world and blessed us with all spiritual blessings. He desires that those who believe in His holy name should live a holy and blameless life before Him in love.[4] Paul wrote to the Christians at Ephesus to encourage them to pay heed to these spiritual advices and live a blameless life. Christian holiness is often misconstrued; it is not an absolute perfection that belongs to God alone, nor is it angelic perfection—nor is it Adamic perfection—for no doubt Adam had a perfect head and a perfect heart before he sinned against God. Christian holiness is a state of heart and life that consists of being and doing all the time not by breaks and starts, but steadily, just what God wants us to be and do. [5]

Holiness does not mean straightjacket godliness or isolation from people. It means that we are set apart or consecrated to live as a living witness to the Holy God while we live in the world—be in the world, but be not of the world. The Bible says, be holy just as I am holy. The genuineness of our holiness must be simply seen by our day-to-day living and dealing with people.

I have presided at many Methodist Annual Conferences. At these conferences, it has become a routine and meaningless exercise to find out whether ministers are blameless in their official relations and conduct. The answer has always been deceptively positive. We can be blameless before our fellow-Christians, but certainly not before Jesus. Our holy claims must match the way we live.

It was God's dream to restore the broken relationship with man by giving him sonship through adoption in Jesus. We were alien, stranger to God and His immeasurable riches, because of our inclination to sin. But God sent His only begotten Son, our Lord Jesus, into the world to die for our sins on the Cross, so that we may receive adoption as His children. [6] This was not understood by the so-called followers of the Law—the Pharisees, whom Jesus called the children of Satan. [7] They were more interested in ritual, tradition and outward form of cleanliness rather than inward holiness. Jesus called them whitewashed tombs! We are not inheriting eternal and immeasurable riches and imprint of God's image because of our tendency to sin.

He Revealed in Jesus

The mystery of His dream was revealed in Jesus. The Bible tells us that in the past God spoke to our ancestors in many and various ways through the prophets, but in these last days He has spoken to us through His Son.[8] God revealed His dream in all wisdom.[9] It is an all-inclusive revelation; nothing was hidden or kept secret for the future. We hardly make any difference between knowledge and wisdom, but there is. Knowledge is the storehouse of information and its application is wisdom. We have knowledge about God, the Son and the Holy Spirit as given in the Bible. It is necessary for us to know one true, invisible and eternal God, who revealed Himself in Jesus, but it is not sufficient; its application to experiencing God's power in our life is vital for our living.

God's dream is revealed in all insights or hidden truth—
the plan of salvation for humanity. It is inclusive of Jesus'
birth, His death, the resurrection, the ascension and the
second coming. It was the will of the Almighty God to lead
people from darkness to the ultimate truth.

He Fulfilled in Jesus

The fulfilment of God's dream is the hallmark of Christian
faith. If God's dream was not fulfilled in Jesus, our faith in
Him could have been in vain. This was the only way in
which God's own broken image in man could be restored.

He saved and appointed us to live for His praise and
glory. [10] Many of us still live for our own praise, not at all
mindful of the truth that we are called from darkness to
light to bear witness to the Light of the world, to live for His
praise and glory. We are very anxious to hear good words
of praise and honour from men around us. But we make a
very little or no efforts to live for His praise and glory.

The Church is in a mess, struggling to live on wrong
values, making falsehood and injustice as its prestige issues.
The Church must remember the words of Paul, who said,
I regard everything as loss because of the surpassing worth
of knowing Jesus my Lord, to follow Him as my Lord. [11]
Let us then, who are mature, be of the same mind.

God's dream is fulfilled by sending the promised Holy
Spirit. On the day of Pentecost, the early church experienced
the power of the Holy Spirit; the Holy Spirit removed their
fear and filled them with amazement and boldness. They
became witnesses to the risen Lord Jesus Christ—beginning
from their hometown to distant parts of the world. They

were preaching the gospel, doing wonders and miracles and reflecting the imprint of God's image.

There is a story about a king who was very keen to find a talent in his kingdom. He made an announcement throughout his kingdom to bring all artists together who could take part in a painting competition. At the appointed time all assembled; at the end two were selected. The king was to decide who was the best between them. They were given walls facing each other in a big hall to do their painting.

One of the artists began to clean the surface of the wall and mix colours. After some time, he looked back to see what his competitor was doing. He was taken aback to see that he was still smoothing the surface of the wall. He suspected his competitor may copy his painting. So, he brought it to the notice of the king. The king ordered to put a curtain between them. He began to give final touches to his painting, while the other was still smoothing the wall.

When the time was over, the king looked at the paintings. He was unable to decide which one was the original painting, as there was a perfect reflection of the painting on the other wall.

We are sealed with the promised Holy Spirit. The seal has been always the sign of authority, ownership, safety and security. The seal of the Holy Spirit is the guarantee of our spiritual inheritance and acquired possession of His Son, our Lord Jesus. We are made in God's image and owned by Him by paying the ransom for our sins. He sealed us by the promised Holy Spirit to live for His praise and glory.

I was presented a book on Nelson Mandela. The foreword was written by President Bill Clinton and U.N.

Secretary-General Kofi Annan. Nelson Mandela had a dream for a free and democratic South Africa. He was imprisoned for 27 years and endured isolation and physical suffering for his struggle for freedom, equality and human dignity. But he kept his dream alive. On 27 April 1994, Nelson Mandela became the first black President of South Africa; later he also won the Nobel Peace Prize.

Some of you have already achieved your dream, while others are still dreaming and working hard to achieve it. God, too, has an eternal and everlasting dream for you.

References: (1) Gen.3: 15 (2) Gen.1: 26 (3) Heb. 10:2 (4) Eph.1: 4 (5) Brangle, Help to Holiness, p.3 (6) Gal.4: 5 (7) Jn.8: 44 (8) Heb.1: 2 (9) Eph.1: 8f (10) Eph.1: 12 (11) Phil.3: 8

CHAPTER 17

Power of Small Things

Small things are often considered insignificant, useless and undesirable. A huge crowd was following Jesus because the people in it saw Him healing the sick and doing great signs. When Jesus was sitting at the mountainside with His disciples, he saw the large crowd coming to Him. He said to Philip, give them something to eat? Jesus said this to test him, for He knew what He was going to do. But Philip said to the Lord, how are we to buy bread for so many people to eat? Six months' wages (equivalent to about 200 pennies) would not be sufficient to buy enough food for them. Just at that moment, Andrew said to Jesus, there is a boy who has five barley loaves and two fish, but what they among so many? Certainly, it is not sufficient for so many people when we see through human eyes! [1] We do think in the same way as Philip and Andrew; seldom we realise that Jesus can multiply few or small things and turn them into a power.

Remember, small things, too, can turn into big things. Walt Disney, a great cartoonist, was publicly criticised and rejected in the early days of his career. One day, the pastor of a church asked him to draw some cartoons for his church. When he was drawing a picture of a small rodent-infested shed near the church, he saw a small mouse. The sight inspired him to draw a new cartoon. That was how Mickey Mouse was born.

Small in Size

Small things are normally considered powerless and unwanted. But Jesus tells us that there is great power and energy in small things as well. While teaching a lesson on the Kingdom of God, Jesus said that a mustard seed is the smallest of all seeds, but it can grow into a tree.[2] All big and powerful things have small beginnings.

King Saul felt helpless against the Philistines who had gathered for a battle at Socoh, a mountainous area. Goliath of Gath, who was six cubits (about nine feet) tall with the body structure of a giant, led the Philistines. David, the youngest son of Jesse, convinced King Saul to allow him to fight with Goliath. King Saul offered David his armour and sword, but David was too small to use them. When Goliath saw David, he ridiculed him, for he was only a youth, ruddy and handsome in appearance. Goliath felt insulted. He said to David, "Am I a dog that you come to me with sticks?" David put a small smooth stone in his sling and swung the stone at Goliath. The stone pierced Goliath's forehead and he fell flat. David could overpower Goliath because he had given himself into the hand of God. [3]

God gave enormous physical strength to Samson. The angel of the Lord appeared to Samson's mother, who was barren. He said to her that she would bear a child, that no razor shall come on his head and that the boy shall be a Nazarene. God had locked great strength in Samson's hair. He killed a lion with his bare hands, and later killed 1,000 Philistines with a jawbone of a donkey. But he was deceived; he revealed the secret of his strength to Delilah, who cunningly shaved off his hair. As a result, Samson lost all his strength. [4]

A small computer microchip has the capability to store up an entire encyclopaedia. Electrons can produce a huge quantity of electricity, and a remote control device can guide a big space mission. A small anchor docks a huge ship. The tongue, which is one of the small parts of the human body, can ruin a family, friendship and fraternity. [5] A great forest is set ablaze by a small fire. A small matchstick can cause a great damage. Such are God's ways to show the power of small things in His creation. Jesus wanted His disciples to understand that they can turn small things into powerful things if they believed in Him.

Small in Number

There was a boy who had five barley loaves and two fish. Perhaps, he was shepherding his sheep; his mother might have packed them up for his lunch. Jesus asked His disciples to get the five loaves and the two fish from the little boy, who was so glad to do so. The disciples were perplexed when Jesus said, make the crowd sit for food; they thought that there was not enough to feed such a large crowd. Jesus took the five loaves and the two fish gave thanks and distributed them among those who were seated—this has a reference to the bread from heaven given to the Israelites in the deserts and the Lord's Supper. It was an incredible sight! All ate plentiful and a huge leftover—measuring full twelve baskets—was gathered by the disciples. This was something unusual. They testified that Jesus was indeed the prophet who was to come into the world. They wanted to crown Jesus as their king, but He escaped to the mountain.

God can multiply a small number of things or infuse power in them. We think in terms of our mathematics, but God's mathematics is simply strange. For Jesus, it was 5+2 =5,000 and plus. Do not always insist on a large number; it may mean nothing to God. God always uses a few things to manifest His power.

There is yet another miracle in the Bible. A man from Baalshalishah got the first fruit of his crop, 20 barley loaves and fresh ears of grain. The Prophet Elisha told him to give them to the people to eat, but he responded to the man of God, how can I set this before a hundred people. But the prophet said to do it. The man gave them the barley loaves and the ears of grain to eat, which was enough. [6]

Gideon took 22,000 troops to fight with Midianites, but the Lord said to Gideon, you are having too many troops. Gideon reduced them to 10,000, but the Lord again said to him that they are still too many. Gideon separated the remaining troops between two groups—those who lapped water with their tongues like a dog and those who kneeled down to drink, putting their hands to their mouths. Only 300 troops who lapped were taken by Gideon to fight with the Midianites; they triumphed over their enemies. [7]

David made the mistake of depending on his armed forces. He ordered to take the census of it. God, who gave him victories over his enemies, did not like it. God struck him; he began to pray to God for forgiveness. God gave him three options. Three years of famine or 3 months to flee before his enemies while they pursue him, or 3 days of pestilence throughout his kingdom. David felt safe to fall into the hand of the Lord, for he said His mercy is great. [8]

Of course, number does not matter to those who believe in the power of God.

Small in Status

God called people who had humble origin. But this does not mean that the people from the higher strata of society were unwanted. All are equal before God. The Lord often chose the ones who were of humble origin to manifest His power and mould them in His own plan as the potter shapes a pot out of clay. According to the Bible, "But God hath chosen the foolish things of the world to put to shame the wise, and God has chosen the weak things of the world to put to shame the things which are mighty; and the base things of the world and the things which are despised God has chosen, and the things which are not, to bring to nothing the things that are, that no flesh should glory in His presence." [9]

God chose Rehab the prostitute, who gave shelter to those who came to spy over Jericho. [10] Jesus chose ordinary fishermen of Galilee so that they could tell the story of salvation. He went to the house of a tax collector who was looked down by the members of his own community. Zacchaeus stood before Jesus; he announced, "half of his wealth he will give to poor, and if he has defrauded anyone he would pay back four fold." [11] He chose to talk to a Samaritan woman although Jews had no dealing with Samaritans; at the end of the conversation, she realised that she was speaking to the Messiah. [12]

God sent His only Son into this world; of course, not to be born in a king's palace, but in an ordinary carpenter's family. God chose to be with ordinary people so that they could stand against injustices with the power of the Almighty. In fact, God sets His eyes on the things He desires. God looks at the heart of a person, no matter how small or big the person may be, and chooses him or her out of millions. Feeding the large crowd was not of any big concern to Jesus, but the lack of faith of His disciples in Him was.

Christopher Reeves, who played superman, fell off his horse while riding on it and broke his spinal cord. He was confined to a wheelchair. The actor was fighting depression, but had unquenched zeal for raising funds for his injury treatment. There was little prospect of finding treatment, but he said that when John Kennedy promised that by the end of 1960s we would put a man on the moon, everybody including the scientists shook their heads in dismay, but we did it. He said that we could cure the spinal cord injury, too; if there is a will, there is a way. What was possible in outer space is possible in inner space as well. [13]

It is not easy to believe in the power of small things because small things are too simple. But Jesus used small, simple and few things and turned them into incredible power to manifest His glory, so that the world may believe in Him.

References: (1) Jn.6: 1-14 cf Matt. 15:33 (2) Matt.13: 32 cf. Zech. 4:10 (3) 1 Sam.Chap.17: 37 &50f (4) Judg.16: 19 (5) Jam.3: 6 (6) 2 King 4:42ff (7) Judg.7: 7 (8) 2 Sam. 24:14 (9) 1 Cor.1: 27f (10) Josh. 2:6 &15 (11) Lk.19: 8 (12) Jn.4: 26 (13) Time (Magazine) Aug.26, 1996, p.31

CHAPTER 18

Throw the First Stone

There are Christians all over world who have a holier-than-thou attitude. They regard their fellow Christians as inferior to their own spirituality while concealing their sins. You may expect a series of questions from them that can embarrass you spiritually. Jesus disapproved of the spiritual attitude of the religious leaders of His day.

Taking the woman who was caught in act of adultery to Jesus is a record of a genuine incident in His life.[1] As per the Mosaic Law, punishment for adultery was death by stoning. The Jewish method of execution was to throw a criminal—half naked and with hands tied at the back—from a 10- or 12-foot scaffold. The witness did the pushing with great force; if this did not kill the criminal, the witness would take a large stone and dash it upon the criminal's breast. When a mob stoned a criminal, no scaffold was used. The accuser threw the first stone and then all could throw stones until the criminal was dead. [2]

The scribes and Pharisees brought the woman to Jesus, not so much to get His consent to put her to death by stoning as per the Mosaic Law, but rather to test Him whether He would have any respect for it.

Pseudo-Spirituality

The woman who was caught in the act of adultery was brought before Jesus, but the man was left out. Were they partial? No answer is given. In Biblical times, the act of adultery was seriously viewed as it was considered unlawful; therefore, it was prohibited. [3] The penalty for this offence was death by stoning. [4] Even today, there is social control on it, or else our society may turn into Sodom and Gomorrah in the midst of growing permissiveness among certain groups, even in some sections of the Church.

The scribes and Pharisees were concerned more about the external act of adultery, but Jesus gave them a different understanding of adultery—that even the lust of the eyes is adultery of the heart. [5] Jesus was taking them to a higher and true order of internal cleanliness rather than external cleanliness. Jesus as the Lord has authority to introduce a new provision to the Mosaic Law and set higher spiritual laws. But there is no way or indication that the evil of adultery could be minimised. In that true sense, those who brought the woman to Jesus were guilty of the same as much as the woman; both deserved punishment.

Some time ago, I heard the testimony of a young preacher who surrendered his life to Christ. He said that while he was in the seminary, the principal of the college made an announcement that he had kept the complaint box in the chapel. If anyone had any complaint against anyone, it could be dropped in the box. The principal added: You don't have to write your name on it. The preacher said he was dead against the evangelical hypocrisy at the college, but as he was writing it down his inner voice spoke to him, "I too have the same complaint against you." The preacher said that he would not write the complaint as he was not worthy of condemning others, because he was not flawless himself.

With unspoken words, Jesus was telling those who had brought the woman that they were not sinless to judge her. God gave the Laws through Moses to the people of Israel to maintain the health of society. But it was unfortunate that the scribes and Pharisees began to strictly apply these laws to others. They were more concerned about the letter of the law rather than the spirit of the law. Jesus reminded them that Moses gave these laws because of the hardness of their hearts. They did not realise that man is not made for the law, but the law is made for man's welfare. [6]

Jesus wanted them to follow all Mosaic Laws, not only the ones that suited them the most. He reminded them how craftily they evaded their responsibility of supporting their parents by declaring proportionate amount of support as 'corban' to God under the pretext of their tradition. [7] Jesus spoke to them on several occasions that external cleanliness is good, but inner or spiritual cleanliness is what God looks at.

The scribes and Pharisees, zealous followers of laws and religious leaders should set spiritual standards for themselves first, before they apply them to others. But in practice it was vice-versa. They applied these standards to others, not to themselves. Jesus said to them, "How can you say to your neighbour, 'let me take the speck out of your eye', while the log is in your eye?" [8] It is unfortunate, hypocrites magnify insignificant mistakes of others with the intention to condemn and punish others, while they conceal their own mountainous sins.

Jesus was concerned about such pseudo-spirituality of the scribes and Pharisees. He described them as whitewashed tombs. [9] Such pseudo-spirituality is crippling the Church's ministry to the world more than external forces.

Self-Righteousness
Jesus always said that social outcasts, publicans and sinners were nearer to the Kingdom of Heaven than the hypocrites among religious leadership. [10] While the scribes and Pharisees were constantly questioning Jesus, He hoped that they should realise their own spiritual bankruptcy first. When people are infected with revenge and self–righteousness; they become blind to their own follies. Jesus knew that they were far from being perfect and yet pressing Him to condemn and perform the magisterial role.

Contrary to their expectation, Jesus put the spiritual challenge before them. He said to them, "If any one among you has committed no sin should throw the first stone at her." Although they were religious leaders, dressed in ceremonial robes, they could not throw the first stone at her.

I remember on several occasions the religious leaders of my church quarrelled with one another over their blunders. They came to meetings full of stones, but left without using them, as they were guiltier of many serious charges than the person they were implicating. Mind you, they merely deferred to use them, but never discarded the thought of using them again, waiting for a favourable opportunity.

Self-righteousness has taken deep roots in our church system. It has become the accepted lifestyle for many religious leaders. They tend to live a double life—public life and private life. A preacher illustrated it so beautifully. He said that once a pastor was giving an evangelistic sermon in his church. He spoke very well, and the members of his congregation responded spontaneously and overwhelmingly to the Alter call. Among those who responded to the Alter call were his wife and their children. After the prayer, his wife and their children stayed back. The pastor asked her, "What are you doing here"? She said to her husband, "You look so good in the pulpit; let us make our home here." Jesus was condemning such self-rigorousness of the scribes and Pharisees who brought the woman who was caught in the act of adultery. Jesus wanted them to consider their own spiritual condition first, before they could condemn the woman.

Let us search our own hearts first, before we can throw the first stone at others. David, in one of his psalms, prayed, "Search me, O God, and know my heart; test me and know my thought. See, if there is any wicked way in me, and lead me in the everlasting way." [11] Let us be honest before our God; we cannot hide anything from Him. Remember, self-righteousness leads to destruction, but Christ-like righteousness though difficult leads us to eternal life. Let us not hold the outward form of godliness while denying its power.[12] Put away every spiritual pretension before condemning any one of our brothers. For the measure you give will be the measure you get. [13]

Neither Do I Condemn You

Jesus wanted the self-righteous scribes and Pharisees to face a simple yet profound spiritual challenge—if you are without sin. They came to Jesus with ill intention to put Him in a trap, but Jesus knew what was in their hearts. It was a very tricky situation. Had Jesus contradicted the Mosaic Law, they could have condemned Him as a false prophet. Jesus respected the laws; therefore, He said, "I did not come into this world to abolish the law, but to fulfil it." [14] And had He condemned the woman who was caught in the act adultery, He would have been accused by them for usurping the Roman authority.

He never bypassed any authority or exercise extra authority, or abused His authority as the only Begotten Son of the Father. He said, "Give to Caesar that belongs to Caesar and to God that belongs to God." [15] He did not come to abolish the Law or prophets, but to fulfil. [16]. More importantly, as New Moses, He had authority to give a new Law. He bent down; perhaps He wrote the new Law with His fingers on the stony ground, 'if you are sinless, throw the first stone'. This was a befitting reply. He bent down the second time and wrote on the ground. Nothing is known what Jesus wrote. But it made the self-righteous scribes and Pharisees feel small before God's righteousness. He perhaps wrote all kinds of sins they were nurturing in their hearts—jealousy, enmity, hatred and conspiracy, including adultery, etc. Those who gathered around the woman to stone her, left silently one by one while He was writing on the ground. Only Jesus and the woman who was brought to Him were left. Although, the scribes and Pharisees fell short of God's standard of righteousness, their conscience was not dead like many of us. They quietly conceded the fact that they were not worthy to throw the first stone.

Today, the situation in the Church is just the opposite; people with all kinds of vices are throwing the first stone; Jesus' message of love and forgiveness makes no sense to them. The conscience of most church leaders is dead; they are always ready to rub the wrong side. The Word of God falls on their deaf ears. They are like royal guests at a banquet, but forbidden to eat anything. Some time ago, I was told that the person who was representing to pursue a case against a certain church leader confessed that the so-called allegations were fabricated. There is lack of conscience in the Body of Jesus Christ; many Christians are not able to rise above it to lead a Christian life as expected by our Lord. Such religious leaders, who have become a black spot on Christianity, are already condemned in the sight of Jesus!

Jesus asked the woman, "Where are they? Has no one condemned you?" She replied, "No one, Sir." Jesus said, "Neither I condemn you; go your way; do not sin again." [17] Jesus was not approving the act of adultery; He came to save men from their sins, not to destroy them if they repented of their sins.

References: (1) Jn.8: 1-11 (2) Num.15: 36 (3) Ex.20: 14, Lev. 18:20 & Deut. 5:18 (4) Deut. 22:23f (5) Matt. 5:28 (6) Deut. 31:27 & Mk. 10:5 (7) Mk.7: 11ff (8) Matt.7: 4 (9) Matt.23: 27 (10) Matt. 5:20 & 21:31 (11) Ps. 139:23f (12) 2 Tim. 3:5 (13) Mark 4:24 (14) Matt.5: 17 (15) Lk.20: 25 (16) Matt. 5: 17 (17) Jn.8: 11

CHAPTER 19

They May Be One

Jesus prayed for His disciples. He prayed, "They may be one, as we are one." [1] This is the greatest prayer ever said. Jesus was concerned about His disciples, not so much for the twelve, but for those who would come after the twelve; lack of harmony among the disciples could have become the main issue. Obviously, the Church has been facing the problem of togetherness or unity right from the early times. Christians are divided on one issue or the other. This is one of the major concerns that take much of our time and energy.

The significance of Christian unity is indisputable from the time of the early church. It has now become all the more important for our co-existence and Christian witness. Unity means oneness or singleness, or individuals constituting one complex whole. Unity does not mean uniformity, though the core values are shared by uniting individuals. The term unity is used in the RSV Bible four times in the sense of harmony within a community. [2] The Psalmist celebrates the beauty of brothers living in unity; it is like the precious oil on the head, running down on the beard—on the beard of Aaron. [3] The New Testament places a strong emphasis on the importance of unity. Paul exhorts Ephesians Christians to maintain unity. [4] In a similar manner, Peter exhorts the early Christians to be "of one mind, having compassion for one another." [5]

The Reality

We know that churches are divided on issues such as sacraments, liturgy and the forms of church governance. The task of achieving oneness within church denominations is difficult, but not impossible.

The various types of group formations do not contribute to integration within a church denomination and between churches. The former is less manifest than the latter. There are many other factors, such as personality type and conflict of interests in terms of power-sharing and desire of one church denomination to gain supremacy over others, that act as dangerous explosives in breaking the unity of the Body of Christ. Nobody ever thought that Jesus' followers would make such rigid boundaries of denominations for themselves. The Indian-American astronaut, Sunita Williams, who spent 195 days, in a space station, said, "There are no borders when you look down from space. You don't see your hometown or the crowded streets. You see the planet's big geographical features, not political separation or countries' borders. Borders exist only on paper and in our minds. The earth looks beautiful from space." [6]

It is disheartening to find that the Church has been experiencing divisions and conflicts from its early days. They do not enhance oneness in Jesus. We are for unity, not for disunity. The divisions and conflicts within church denominations and between churches must disappear. The greatest prayer of Jesus was for unity among His disciples. This was one of the central themes in His life and teachings. To become effective witnesses of our Lord, we should always stand united.

The Scriptures tell us that a kingdom divided against itself will lie waste and that a city or house divided will not stand.[7] Someone rightly said that united we stand and divided we fall. The ever-expanding denominational divisions weaken the unity in the Church, making the Church a soft target. This does not mean that we must show the power of our muscles, not the strength of our unity in Christ. Let us not emphasise the superiority of one church denomination over the other or one person over the other. The Corinthians were claiming that they belonged to Paul or Apollos, or Cephas, or Christ. Paul disapproved it; he questioned them as to how they could divide Christ. [8]

Sanctify In Truth
Jesus prayed that His disciples might be sanctified in the truth. The value of truthfulness is something that is often considered in the Church, but rarely practised. This is a dilemma that looms large in the Church today. The vested interest groups in the Church intentionally conceal the truth; the church annual reports and statistics do not give a true picture of the state of the Church.

I met a person who had run away from his family when he was 11 years old. Ever since then he had been living in Mumbai. In 1972, when he was desperate, lonely and had nothing on him, he found a wallet containing Rs 14,000 in a taxi he had hired. He could have kept quiet about it, but he informed the taxi driver in his truthfulness. The taxi driver told him that it was for the first time after a three-day break that he was driving the taxi. He also told the man that he should keep the wallet as he had found it. Many would say that truthfulness does not pay any more, but it does. Remember, truthfulness pays in the long run.

Today, a number of people in the Church are undergoing traumas because of the falsehood practiced by the so-called church leaders. Galileo advocated the Copernican system, which held the view that the solar system is centred on the sun with the earth and other planets revolving around it. This enraged the Jesuits; it was declared false and erroneous by the Church in 1616. He was tried and found guilty of heresy; so he was forced to declare it erroneous. He was kept under house arrest till the end of his life. Recently, the Roman Catholic Church apologised for making such a big mistake, but the harm done to Galileo cannot be undone.

Some Christians believe that one is not rewarded in this world if one practises the truth. There is an urgent need to change our mindset. Jesus prayed for His disciples to be cleansed in the truth. You need to be truthful if you wish to follow Jesus. Pontius Pilate knew that Jesus was innocent, and yet he asked Jesus what truth was. Everyone wants to know the truth, but when truth becomes inconvenient, they do not follow it. Jesus said, "I am the Truth...." The truth is personified in Jesus. Jesus prayed that His disciples too must know the truth and hold fast to it to experience oneness in Him and among them.

The World May Know

We are called by our Lord Jesus to be a guide to the world. The world cannot set an agenda for us, for we can have no other agenda than the one given to us by our Lord: 'You shall be my witnesses to lead peoples of nations to the Light of Life—Jesus Christ'. Jesus prayed that the disciples might be one, so the world may know that Jesus is the Saviour of the world. Jesus called His disciples and sent them to preach, teach and witness to the whole world. The early church was faithful to God's command. It went out with the redemptive story of Jesus. The gospel first tended to remain confined to the Jews, but it soon broke the barrier of cultures and geography. It began to move out of Jerusalem to all parts of the world. There has been hostility towards the gospel, but the preaching of the gospel did not cease. The gospel should be preached in all situations; it is better preached by our deeds, not by our words.

As the Church became more structured and ecclesiastical, the urgency of preaching the gospel did not gather much importance. The Church is pre-occupied with many non-issues. It is said that the Church of England overlooked the request of China to send 100 missionaries as the Church was involved in who's who; so a great opportunity to preach the gospel was lost. Jesus prayed for unity among His disciples, so the world may believe in Him. How can we make the world believe in Jesus when we do not show unity in the Spirit of the Lord and indulge in partisan spirit? The core message of the gospel is reconciliation between God and man, initiating all believers into the Kingdom of God—a melting pot in Jesus. I believe that preaching, teaching and effective witnessing are both the cause and effect of the unity of the Body of Jesus Christ.

It is believed that St. Thomas came to India with the gospel. The first church was started in South India, but it remained, more or less, stationary until foreign missionaries arrived on the Indian soil. Different denominational churches were started; they began to grow, but soon became sleeping giants. This tendency is seen all over the world. The task of evangelisation is now more vigorously pursued by those who belong to various churches—who are not part of the Church's organisational set-up. They are making a significant contribution, pushing up the curve in the conversion graph; others only steal sheep from mainline churches to inflate figures and serve selfish motives.

Cultural and racial diversity and differences in individuals' capabilities in the Church are noticeable. But we all believe in the same Lord. No one is greater or bigger, or indispensable, in the sight of our Lord. In Jesus, we are freed and united. This is the moment of inclusiveness for all those who believe in his name, resulting in the experience of Christ's shared values. The extent to which we will become an inclusive people in Jesus depends on the extent to which we share Christ's values. On the day of Pentecost, this was visible as people belonging to different nationalities and languages began to hear each other in their own native tongue, though they spoke no other language than their own. Let nothing act as a hindrance to oneness in Jesus.

References: (1) Jn.17: 11 (2) Bromiley, Geoffrey W. (ed.), op.cit., Vol. IV p. 947 (3) Ps.133: 1f (4) Eph.4: 3 (5) 1Pet.3: 8 (6) *Times of India*, Mumbai, 7 October 2007, p.5 (7) Matt.12: 25 (8) 1Cor.1: 12

CHAPTER 20

The Best Is Yet to Come

Some church leaders claim that they are the ones who should lead the Church. They assert their right at every available opportunity in the Church and try hard to make it difficult for better people to assume leadership positions in the Church. They nurture the idea that they are indispensable. But, as we all know, egoists are unfit to take forward Jesus' message of humility. Their claim that only *they* can lead the Church undermines the power of God and ignores the words of Jesus—don't you know that God was able to raise children for Abraham out of stones? We are no one to limit God's power to raise leaders; our self serving interests can never change the way God thinks and chooses a leader to lead His flock. It is a fallacy to say that we are the best, for the best is yet to come.

In the second chapter of the Gospel according to St. John, we read that Jesus was present at the wedding feast at Cana. The guests were served with wine, but soon it got over. Jesus asked the servants at the feast to fill the jars with water; then He asked them to draw some from it and give it to the master of the feast. When the master of the feast had tasted the water that was made wine, and did not know where it came from, the master of the feast said to the bridegroom: "Every man at the beginning sets out the good wine, and when the guests have well drunk, then that which is inferior; but you have kept the good wine until now." God works miracles; He gives us the best of things during difficult times. Perhaps, we are not the best Christians or leaders in the Church, for the best is yet to come!

Scarcity
This was the first miracle that Jesus performed. We are witnessing scarcity of everything everywhere and it may become even more severe in times to come.

The scarcity of raw materials and personnel resources is a widespread cry the world over. Scientists are sending warning to us on the rapid depletion of natural resources. It is said that the world is like a ship sailing on an Ocean, which carries limited supplies for living; supplies need to be used very carefully. Scientists are offering alternate ways to overcome the scarcity of natural resources by recycling used materials and discovering substitute materials to keep the world moving forward in a bigger and better way.

The church, too, is facing the scarcity of committed leaders who can take forward the mission of the Church. The financial resources are lacking, but more importantly visionary leaders who care for God's mission for the perishing world are not found. The Church realises it. There is an urgent need for committed leaders to lead God's mission in our dangerous world. The situation is becoming gloomy, but we trust in God to raise leaders of His choice and provide us with all that is necessary for the extension of His Kingdom.

In Biblical times, the world faced many miserable situations, but the Almighty raised men of God to deal with them. Jeremiah the prophet was chosen to have power over nations and kingdoms and to cause rise and fall of kingdoms. [1] It was in scarcity of things that God did miracles. There are many who aspire for leadership position in the Church, but only a few of them are willing to be leaders after the heart of God; for instance, King David. In the present situation, the Church needs leaders who seek nothing but God's Kingdom and His righteousness, deny self and serve His people. Indeed, God will raise leaders who will match His expectation for the Church's ministry.

God always works miracles and provides the best things during hard times. The best of inventions and discoveries were made in times of need. God provided manna as food when there was no food to eat in the wilderness; a rock was struck to quench the thirst of those who rebelled against Moses. The widow of Zarephath fed Elijah; the meal in the jar and the oil in the jug did not go dry until the day that the Lord sent rain on earth. [2] God always acts in times of crisis. If you are facing a crisis, do not be scared, for the loving God will always be with you to give you the best. God raises the best men and women to lead His sheep in evergreen pastures—to make us experience the abundance of His resources.

In the early eighteenth century, there was a spiritual crisis in England. There was worldliness among the clergy; every sixth house in London was a public house, displaying signs and informing customers that they could get drunk for a penny. In those times of crisis, God raised John Wesley, who began to preach tirelessly to save souls from perishing. He began to look upon the world as his parish. For fifty years he preached almost daily to crowds of five to twenty thousand people. During his ministry, he travelled 250,000 miles and gave 40,000 sermons. [3]

Simplicity

Jesus could turn water into wine. Water is a simple element; it is easily available. There was no delay in filling the six water jars with potable water. Today potable water is not so easily available for the growing population the world over. There are people in many Indian villages and other parts of the world who go to distance places to fetch potable water. Water has become a major political weapon in many countries around the world.

God always used ordinary things and people; He turned them into extraordinary ones. He chose the foolish things of the world to confound the wise. Jesus chose the simple fishermen of Galilee and turned them into extraordinary people, who in turn turned the world upside down. God manifested His powers by using simple things; He made them the best in times of crisis. King Saul was chosen from the least clan of Benjaminite, the smallest tribe of Israel, and the humblest of all the families of the tribe. David, the simplest and youngest among the sons of Jesse, was anointed by God to be the King of Israel. Moses was not useful to God until he was made simple and humble, and Paul became a powerful instrument of the Lord, only when he stepped down to the ordinary rank.

Christians in the early church and missionaries reached
with the gospel first to the lower strata of the society, who
were more approachable and acceptable to the message of
salvation in Jesus. Paul wrote to the church at Corinth that
many of them were not powerful and belonged to a noble
class. [4] But be cautious; it must not be construed that the
gospel is meant only for the lower strata of society, the
unintelligent people of the world. The message of the gospel
is for all people of the world, for all have sinned and fallen
short of the glory of God.

There is strength in simplicity. There are numerous world
leaders who lived simply and identified themselves with
the masses to free them from poverty, oppression and
human indignity. Mahatma Gandhi, Martin Luther King Jr.
and Nelson Mandela are some outstanding examples. Jesus
cared for the suffering ones and those who were looked
down upon. He showed the Way of life, for He Himself was
the Way, the Truth and the Life. Simplicity is the essence of
greatness. It does not mean 'stupidity' or 'worthless things'.
It was the style of Jesus' teachings; He always led people
from things simple and familiar to things complex and
invaluable.

Superiority
In the above-mentioned miracle, water was turned into not
just wine, but superior wine. The master of the feast said,
"You have served the inferior wine first and kept the good
wine till the last." But the best has a price.

We need to pay the price of obedience. The mother of
Jesus told servants to do whatever Jesus asked them to do.
There must be implicit obedience. God asked Abraham to

offer his son to Him as a burnt offering; Abraham simply obeyed God. It was a very heart-breaking situation, but he did not argue with God. He offered his son, Isaac, to God as a burnt offering. The lad looked up at his father's face and said to him, "Father, I see the wood and the fire, but where is the lamb for a burnt offering?" "The Lord will provide," replied Abraham. [5] He was about to slit his son's throat, but his unwavering obedience performed a miracle. God asked him not to lay his hand on his son; He sent a lamb for a burnt offering. The best things flow into our life when we are obedient to the living God in times of crisis.

However, the best things may not come to us instantly. The miracle of turning water into wine was not performed at the wish of the bridegroom's servants at the marriage feast, though they felt panicky about the shortage of wine. They expected an uninterrupted supply of wine to the guests. The Lord was told about it; He showed no sign of anxiety, but simply said that His time would come. The best things normally come at God's appointed time—not instantly. Some thought that by the time His time came, everything would be over, but no! His time came before the wedding feast ended.

God wants us to be patient to experience the power of His words, for patience is power! It is said, patience is a bitter plant that bears sweet fruits. Let us not be anxious about the crises in our life or scarcity of Spirit-filled church leaders or church finances, but wait on Him as God's chosen children, for He will turn our unhappiness into happiness in His own time.

Jesus neither said a word nor touched the water jar. He just prayed over it. The best thing simply came at the command of His words. Jesus turned the ordinary water into extraordinary wine to make us believe that He holds the universe in his hands. He created the laws of the universe; they are subject to Him. The disciples who followed Jesus were looking for some signs like the Jews to believe that He was the Son of the Living God; so Jesus did the same to reveal His glory. [6]

We may be the right people for church leadership, but we cannot claim that we are the best ones in the sight of God to seek the lost and lead them. We are not the best church leaders, for the best is yet to come to save the souls from perishing. The words of John the Baptist are relevant in this context. He said, "It is He who, coming after me, is preferred before me, whose sandal strap I am not worthy to loose." [7] We may be good Christians, but not the best in the sight of God. The best is yet to come! God can surely raise the best Christians and church leaders. Let us patiently wait to witness God's miracle!

References: (1) Jer. 1: 10ff (2) 1 King 17:16 (3) Allen, William E., op. cit. p. 5 (4) 1Cor.1: 26 (5) Gen. 22:8 (6) Jn. 2:11 (7) Jn.1: 27